Vivienne Neville

Set Adrift

Former Clergy Wives Speak Out

Working Towards An Adequate
"National Care Policy" In the Church of England
For Clergy Spouses And Their Children

© 2019 «Set Adrift»
Vivienne Neville

Edited By:
Vivienne Neville
Katharine Harrison
Grateful Advice From Stuart Bexon
Further Editing By
Margo Coser

ISBN 978-1-9164983-0-3
Published By VJM Media Publishing
Vivienne Neville
www.vivneville.com

Typesetting by UK Book Publishing
www.ukbookpublishing.com

Cover by Michael Gant
Rainbow Photography
www.rainbowphoto.co.uk

Agent Contact: Jackie Bates
Nashville Tennessee
jackiebates@icloud.com

This Book Is Dedicated To

My Precious Parents Henry and Margo.

Siblings and Extended Family

My Heartfelt Thanks To You All

I'm sorry I didn't tell you the full extent of my plight at times. It took a while for me to be able to share fully. I love you all so much.

To All Who Have Supported Me Especially In Prayer On This Journey

Jackie, Lloyd, Betty, James, Liz, Ian, Michael, Brenda, Pastor Jordan, Pastor Eve, Pastor Rikki, Ros, Elspeth, David, Jacqui, Pete, Alison, Pastor Cliff, Pastor Luke, Natalie, Cath, Gill, Andrew, Mark, Andrew, Eileen, Karen, Julia, Ian, Peggy, Olwyn, Trisha, Sam, Stephen, Tara, Mary, David, Geoff, Jenny, Lorraine, Jason, Lisa, Linda and more, thank you.

Thank You To All At "Broken Rites" Clergy Spouses

You Are The Most Wonderful Caring People

Who Are Very Brave. You Are My Heroes.

Contents

Endorsements

"It was revelational for me to read about the pervasive problem of marital breakdown/separation/divorce among clergy in the Church of England - but heartbreaking to read about the lack of love and care given to the clergy-families: of overnight loss of husband, home, job, church. Vivienne Neville author of "Set Adrift" highlights this grievous issue, and bravely calls for redress of the Church often turning a blind eye. History tells us God raises up reformers to address societal injustices and right wrongs - like Martin Luther and William Tyndale - which requires great courage. My prayer is that the victims will fearlessly come forward - that the whole truth will be heard - and that the Church and public policy will respond bravely, replacing an antiquated and unfair system, with an adequate and safe care policy on behalf of the vulnerable: the spouses and children".

Bob Farrell (Author of "I Will Be")

"To challenge the perceived authority of the church's hierarchy has historically been taboo - this book now heralds the start of change"
Anon

"Viv's book reveals the often-hidden experiences and difficulties that are faced by clergy spouses and partners many of whom do feel that they are indeed 'set adrift' when a relationship breaks down. We at Broken Rites are committed to working with the churches to help alleviate these problems".

Margaret Wilkinson and Dilys Stone (Broken Rites Chair & Vice Chair)

The lid has finally been lifted off this dreadful issue in the Church of England. It's been bubbling and simmering for over 35 years. It is time to hear the truth and the experiences of the silent partners of divorced clergy. The suffering of innocent women and children.

There is a right time for everything, and it is the right time for "Set Adrift" to be published. Vivienne is a brave God-fearing woman with a very large loving heart and GOD is with her every step of the way and he will carry her through when extra protection is needed.

Solveig Warren (Broken Rites)

Opening Words

For the past two years I have been researching what happens to a clergy spouse and children when a clergy marriage breaks down. As part of a group of 150+ clergy spouses, with 78% from the Church of England, I have been sent many of their accounts of the process they have been through when going through separation and divorce. The reasons for marital breakdown are not the issue here, those reasons are private and between the couple themselves, this book concentrates on the journey of the clergy spouse and children during the separation period and divorce. The following are my findings. Thank you to all who have shared their accounts with me and as a former clergy spouse I also speak from experience.

As a vicar's wife, I shared in the joys and the sorrows of many individuals both within and outside of the church environment. I have listened to countless stories and accounts from people within congregations. Never in my life as a vicar's wife did I ever come across another wife going through marital breakdown who had to leave her home without having another home to go to. I have never known another wife lose her husband overnight, her home, pet, belongings, church family, geographical area, financial security and soon after her job. I have never known anyone experience all those losses at once, except clergy spouses. As stated, I am now part of a group of 150+ clergy wives and two clergy husbands who have experienced some of these losses at once - or all of these major losses at once. Compounded on top of all of this loss is often a lack of support from the church, senior staff and hierarchy; the diocese in which you live, determine the amount of help a clergy spouse and children are given from the church and diocese on marriage breakdown. Your postcode determines the care and love you are shown when a clergy marriage breaks down, as RT Hon Frank Field states in his introduction to the 2018 Broken Rites Annual General Meeting, which you can read a little further on in this book. When clergy marriage breakdown happens, in the majority of cases the decision to end the marriage is made by the clergyman. Your postcode and diocese determine the extent of your safety and provision through this time, not the love, compassion and care of God from individual powerful people in the Church of England. Outside of provisional diocesan postcodes, I can't stress enough how difficult life becomes for the clergy spouse during a clergy marital breakdown. Clergy spouse, you could find yourself homeless if you have not made provision for the future. Please also make sure you have your own personal pension; do not rely on the pension of your spouse or the cash lump sum at retirement. Currently, pension law stipulates that after 30+ years of marriage, clergy spouses are entitled to 50% of their ex partners pension. Regardless of this lawful act we have many accounts of clergy people dominating and controlling the spouse over the amount that they deem acceptable from the pension. If you have the means to pay for a solicitor, they will help you - if you have no means, you are on your own. Your ex-partner will remain financially stable and therefore powerful throughout this time, they will have the help of their solicitor – you could be left with no help. If you are on your own with no solicitor and you ask the Bishop to help you over possessions or money he may or may not help you and will say those issues are for the law to assist you in. You really will be on your own with these major problems.

Clergy spouse do not think this will never happen to you because that is what nearly all clergy spouses thought. So please be wise in the financial provision for you and your children, because if anything does go wrong in your marriage you will enter a nightmare world if you have no financial provision or a home of your own outside of the vicarage. This book contains many factual experiences from clergy spouses in marital difficulties across the Church of England in the UK. No individual names have been given nor will they ever be. Every person connected to this plight has their own load to carry, and their own reasons for doing things. It is not my intention to make any other person's load heavier, but to raise awareness of the very serious issues concerning the plight of clergy spouses and children when marital breakdown occurs. As stated, this book has been collated after two years research from many accounts from members of 'Broken Rites' an organization based in the UK who pastorally support clergy spouses, the majority being clergy wives and a few clergy husbands. 78% of our members are/were clergy spouses from the Church of England.

Psalm 62:8 Oh My people, trust in Him at all times. POUR OUT YOUR HEART to Him, for God is our refuge.

Throughout this book you will be reminded a few times that no one is perfect but despite that fact, God loves us unconditionally.

Clergy Spouses Speak Out

Cover up prolongs the grieving process for the clergy spouse and children. We have to bottle up so much pain on marriage breakdown and not live freely. We all have to decide as individuals what is best for each one of us. Cover up and silence over the truth of marriage breakdown, whatever that reason is most often the clergy person's decision to end the marriage for reasons of their own which are often heartbreaking for the spouse and children. This results in the clergy spouse and children having to slink away in secret from the vicarage and often being told by leadership that they do not need to talk about what's happened. Those who say this to clergy spouses are compounding the abuse of cover up. Let me expand on this a little. It is no one else's business as to the reasons of a marriage breakdown but if a clergy person ends a marriage that truth should be told. Not the reason but the decision to end the marriage.

Jesus only asked a few people not to talk about a few miracles that had happened, but to the leaders of the day He was honest in His words to them, when He did not agree with them, He spoke up, He didn't slink away in silence and secrecy. Sometimes He said direct words to them that they did not like, so much so that they plotted in secrecy to dispose of Him, to get rid of Him, to push Him out of sight. All those words and plans in secret God sees and God hears EL ROI I AM the God who sees you. Clergy person when you make your plans to send your spouse away, when you tell your lies to put yourself in a good light and destroy the reputation of your clergy spouse, God Sees. That is the truth, but the truth in most of these cases is shrouded in secrecy, shrouded in lies, shrouded in hidden conversations and cover up behind closed doors. God is all seeing, all knowing, omnipresent. Meetings, and hushed tones are not secret to Him. We have one place to get things right before we meet Him face to face on our own. That place is here and now. Everything that you lied about or cheated your clergy spouse from, God Knows. You have one place and time to put this right. You hoarded away for yourself and left your wife and children in poverty. You have time to put things right.

Some clergy spouses and children have had to move to unsafe places and been vulnerable to unsafe people. It was your duty to make sure they were safe. Accounts showed that a number of Hierarchy had no compassion on the clergy spouse and her plight, that is fact. Invite the 150+ clergy spouses and speak to us instead of shuttling us away at our lowest and most vulnerable time in our lives. Many of the clergy spouses were not even invited into the same room as a senior representative together with the clergy person breaking up a marriage to discuss what was happening. WHY? The coldness and lack of practical help from senior staff hurt the clergy spouse even further. You are the fathers of the church, and as fathers your role is to care for the whole flock not to cover up when a clergy person is hurting others and causing great suffering to other people. Your role is to show the love, care and compassion of God to all. When a clergy person comes to you with a story about their spouse, speak to all concerned in the situation the clergy person brings to you. Unfortunately, some of your clergy lie, scheme, plan, cheat and cause great damage to their spouses. They are afraid and they are cowards, so they lay all the blame at another person's door. Discern wisely and do not add further to the suffering of the spouse and children.

Until a few years ago I had no idea of the huge national problem and trauma that a lot of clergy spouses and their children had gone through during marital difficulties, separation and divorce. Without being an ex-clergy wife, I would never have known the extent of this problem. Through my experience and the accounts I now have and the research I have done over the past two years, I write this book to help others in the future and hopefully help alongside others towards bringing about an adequate "National Care Policy" In the Church of England and beyond. I and other members of Broken Rites www.brokenrites.co.uk are continuing to work towards changing this issue for future clergy spouses and their children. Most of the clergy spouses have gone through immense pressure in all areas of life in the rebuilding of their lives after a clergy marriage breakdown. Due to the nature of their clergy person's role in the community, they need to be seen as a role model, but unfortunately some of the clergy people are showing one face to the congregations and one to their families behind the scenes. Of all the marriage breakdowns I have researched nearly all were due to the clergy person who then followed through by blaming their wives and spreading the worst of rumors about them and damaging their reputations very badly, beyond repair. I must stress marital breakdown of the group I have researched only equates to 1% of clergy figures. But the lack of care, compassion and help toward the majority is far from satisfactory.

Male Clergy Spouse

Southern Province UK

"When my marriage broke down, "I was evicted from the Rectory I had nowhere to go. I then spent 18 months in a small bedsit before finding a permanent new home. I was given no help from the diocese. At that time I was severely financially challenged. I was surrounded by 'false news' with no right of reply from the hierarchy. She was incredibly dishonest and did not share her concerns and sought to shelter in the 'comfort' of the church. The hierarchy took sides and I wasn't even considered. The Bishop and Archdeacon were not interested and totally inept of their management"

Many of the clergy spouses report that only the clergy person was taken into account. The spouse was not listened to, and then given little or no practical help. Only the clergy person was allowed to present their side to the Bishop and the clergy spouse was not allowed to present their story to the Bishop only in writing.

Introduction

EL ROI "I AM THE GOD WHO SEES YOU" First of all, I would like to thank you for reading this book; I really hope you finish it as it is very important for us to raise awareness and bring about change in the Church of England and other denominations who may need to review their care policy for clergy spouses and children when marriages breakdown. The purpose of this book is twofold:

1. The contents of this book are first to help, support and point the way for the spouses of clergy, pastors and ministers who are going through difficulties in marriage, separation or divorce. Clergy spouse I am going to help you to know that you are not alone. The contents of this book will bring much light, help and advice into your life.

2. The second reason for this book is with the primary purpose and aim to bring about an adequate "National Care Policy For Clergy Spouses and their children in the Church of England" on marital breakdown. If you are a church leader in whatever denomination, I would ask you to look at your own denominational church policy and consider establishing a safe and adequate policy for clergy spouses and their children. Broken Rites the UK organization set up for clergy spouses was established 35 years ago. The aim of the organization was to assist in changing the

present way that the Church of England deal with clergy spouses and their children on separation and divorce. Tied housing was and still is a very serious major issue on marital breakdown. Tied housing causes clergy spouses and their children great difficulty and in some cases trauma on top of a relationship breakdown and everything that goes with that. A percentage of clergy spouses and children have to leave vicarages with no home to go to. A number of clergy spouses over the years have been forced to begin their lives again with no home of their own to go to and no finances or limited means.

As stated, I belong to a group of 150+ clergy spouses all with their own heartbreaking and incredibly difficult stories to tell. One clergy spouse explained life after her marriage broke down as "being pushed away from the establishment very quickly and becoming invisible". Can you as an individual imagine yourself being pushed away from the church quickly and becoming invisible? Imagine going through a marriage breakdown, which is painful enough, and then the church pushes you away, abandon you and show you no love or care. You lose your immediate church family then you are abandoned by those around you in leadership who are supposed to live their lives showing the love of Jesus to each person in the flock. Alongside that abandonment you also have to deal with a husband or wife clergy person abandoning you at times to the street. The way the ending of the relationships happen and what occurs very quickly after that leaves some clergy spouses and children with "Post Traumatic Stress Disorder".

A clergy spouse and children have multiple major losses to cope with all at once. All at Broken Rites understand the impact when "someone loses not just a spouse or partner but their home, their way of life, sense of purpose, their place in the community and sometimes their faith and job". A research project completed in

Australia showed that 93% of pastor's wives lose their faith in God on marriage breakdown and stop going to church. The impact of loss and lack of spousal help, church help, lack of understanding, compassion and empathy from the church system, all contributed sadly in their loss of faith in God.

Many clergy spouses and their children have been utterly broken by clergymen and a system they believed in and committed their lives to for many decades, some up to and beyond 40 years. Many were "Set Adrift" and abandoned by clergy and the establishment.

Quotes From Clergy Spouses

"My husband for many years talked down to me and made me feel very insignificant. Even after many years divorced, he still speaks badly to me and is very disrespectful to me".

"There are always different perspectives, "you must move on," the Bishop said to me. These words were said to me very early on in the separation period. No words of consolation or counselling or help in mending my marriage just words of "moving on" I was astounded and greatly troubled".

"A minister twice divorced, what sort of message does that send to the community, they deserve better".

"It seems as though my husband and his new partner have just ridden off into the proverbial sunset".

"My children after the separation did not want to go to church any longer".

"The separation is like a death but not with pleasant memories to hold on to".

"Separation and divorce is without doubt a bereavement that senior staff and clergy husbands tell you to move on from straight away. "Just get on with your life and move on," they said. They were cold towards me and had no idea of the grieving process I was going through. They showed me not one ounce of care or understanding".

"When I made my marriage vows, I meant them, for better for worse, for richer or poorer, in sickness and in health till death us do part. I felt as though I needed my marriage vows acknowledging but they were just being thrown away".

"The decree absolute arrived through the post, I dared not open it at first. I had no idea what the impact on my life was going to be when I saw that my marriage was over and final. The letter bore no resemblance at all to the sheer magnitude of its significance".

"When I had received prayer for the ties that still bound me to my former clergy marriage, the prayers then gave me the strength to move forward".

"Life's milestones underlined the act of betrayal not just for me but also for my children. It seems so often that we carry the burden while they walk off into the sunset seemingly unperturbed by their children's joys and sorrows".

"We all go through difficulties in life and we are no exception".

"Towards the end of the marriage he left the room or the house each time I entered. I had no idea what was going on. I was very hurt. It emerged he was having an affair. He hadn't given me eye contact for *a long time. I now know all the signs of an affair, I didn't know them back then".*

"Before our marriage ended, he had emotionally left me, why didn't he tell me the truth instead of me forever wondering what I was doing wrong". This was a common quote from the clergy spouses.

"He emotionally left, long before he physically left me".

"I don't have anywhere to live. I asked the Bishop's Visitor to ask the Bishop if it would be possible for me to given temporary accommodation, the answer was no. I can't believe their lack of care, it's all very hurtful and confusing".

"There has been no practical support from the church hierarchy, for my children and myself. I don't know what my housing options are".

"Most of us have experienced the difficulty of housing".

"Every diocese respond differently, but the lack of care is a major theme".

"I was given no support. I needed financial support in the short term, but I received no such help. I was living on the poverty line".

"If you don't have any money you will be entitled to Universal Credit, housing benefit and council tax reduction. You will be put to the top of the housing list and classed as homeless. That is what happened to me".

"I'm sad to say but I didn't get the support I needed from the church hierarchy".

"I was so shocked and going through the grief at the loss of my clergy spouse. I wasn't capable of sorting things out where a place to live was concerned. I approached the diocese, they said "there was no housing stock available". I then saw vicarages to let in my local church news".

"I room surfed for the first year, I didn't know what to do. I had funds for four months' rent and living expenses then nothing after that as I had lost my job".

"The clergy person and the Church of England should give adequate funding to help those of us who have nothing".

"Sometimes when I open my eyes on a morning, I get a shock when I see the tiny bedroom I now have, my only private space for many years. My bed, wardrobe, TV, fridge, office area all in that small space. I'll never have my own home again; I'm too old for a mortgage unless I get one until I'm 75 years old. He has two homes, the vicarage and the home he bought with his new wife".

"We absolutely need an adequate care policy nationally across the denominations".

"On the breakdown of my marriage the Bishop only interviewed my husband". (That is also a common experience)

"I feel I have no power because people in power are blind and deaf to my plight. I feel totally ground down by the diocesan organization".

"The church completely destroyed my life".

"I managed to cope with his new wife cuddling my grandchildren. It's taken me many years to do so".

"Clergymen/women should not be allowed to make their spouse and children homeless. They should support them financially and practically until they are making enough money for a let, and they must make sure that the family they are sending away are safe and secure".

"Brides of clergy are also caught up as brides of Christ. When clergy marriages collapse, it is so hard to hold on to the relationship with Christ, as the behavior of the 'priest' and 'his' church can be so devastating. Is this spiritual abuse post break up?"

"I married a man with a collar and found myself 'collared'. This breakthrough assembly of spousal voices will lay bare some of the devices used in the 'grooming' of the domiciled clergy wife".

"My question has always been who is listening to the voices of the children and spouses' when the minister of God abuses their trust as a father and husband".

"If I think about what I believe in, I believe in a God who honors truth, honesty, mutual accountability and kindness. None of these applied as my over two decades of marriage to a priest fell apart. I felt death would be a kindness".

"I had evidence, a written report and surveillance from a private investigator that my clergy husband was having an affair, but the Bishop's word was final, and he dismissed the evidence".

I was a clergy spouse who unfortunately has now been divorced. The reasons for any marriage breakdown are between the couple. This book and all the accounts are anonymous, and confidentiality to names, places etc. Will not be disclosed. My faith in God reminds me at all times not to point the finger at anyone or to display words of criticism, but I have written truthful, factual accounts. This book is an attempt to raise awareness of very serious safeguarding issues that clergy spouses and their children are facing, and to work towards bringing about change in national care policies wherever they are needed in faith organizations, to adequately protect clergy spouses and children.

Transition From The Vicarage To Civvy Street

When people leave the military or navy, they talk about the transition into civvy street. I understand now how difficult that transition is. Clergy will never understand that transition because once in the system, usually always in the system. All at Broken Rites understand the "Church Bubble"; when that bubble is burst, the transition away from that life is a massive shock to the system. I could write another book on that transitional stage alone.

My story along with aspects of every ex clergy spouse story is harrowing in parts, it is also miraculous in parts, although I won't be dealing with much of my personal story in this book. It is my hope that the present care policy in the Church of England can be examined and revised because it cannot stay the way it is. There are too many people's lives being devastated, and also great safeguarding issues to be taken into account that need updating and addressing. My next book will focus on the miracles of God throughout my plight. This book will focus on the facts, well-being, safety and the protection of the spouse and children when the devastation of separation and divorce occur.

The hierarchical system is constantly turning its back and going silent on the plight of the clergy spouse. When a marriage breaks down the clergy person is circled and protected by colleagues, senior staff and Bishops. Many accounts show a very unfair system in dealing with marriage breakdown. Some diocese are fair to both parties, some diocese are very unfair, and it is these dioceses that we hope will take everything into account, not just the protection of the clergy person, but also the protection and safeguarding of the clergy spouse and children. There has been much injustice towards clergy spouses and many of the hierarchy and clergy know this, but they have to abide by what the Bishop says, regardless of their own conscience before God. We stand before God now in all our decisions. Our trust must only be in God alone, and if something goes against our own conscience then we need to stand on the side of what we believe is right, and not what another person says to us when we know their advice is not good advice. "Evil flourishes when good men do nothing" Distortions of the truth cause great pain for other people's futures especially when those distortions remain in place.

Abuse comes in many forms: physical, emotional, spiritual, sexual, psychological and financial. Many of the clergy spouses have been subjected to a degree of abuse ranging from moderate to severe, we have also been shown the greatest lack of love we have ever experienced in our lives from a number of clergy and hierarchy. I am sure I speak for us all at Broken Rites; I thank God for this caring, loving, supportive group of clergy spouses. I also must add here that we have been shown great love from certain clergy supporting us in our plight, but unable to bring change.

Senior staff and hierarchy deal with you in such a way that they only want the facts and not the emotional side of your story. If you wear your heart on your sleeve and tell your story in full needing real emergency help, at times, little or no action will be taken, and the clergy spouse is dealt with in a very business-like and unemotional cold fashion by a percentage of the hierarchy.

Many clergy spouses have been faced with a total lack of compassion - they have not been heard. Accounts reported that the hierarchy were not interested in the pain and difficulty the spouse was going through, and most of the time they were not given the help they needed. This attitude and paper exercise added greatly to the clergy spouse's distress and burden, due to the cold and closed down attitude towards them that they experienced from people who they really thought were going to hear them and help them in their greatest hour of need. When I requested the accounts from the clergy spouses, they wrote to me with such decorum and grace after living through some very challenging, difficult, abusive and often heartbreaking circumstances. As sad as marital breakdown is, the majority of the spouses wanted to make their marriages work.

What has shocked me the most while collating this evidence is the effect that separation and divorce has had on the children. Some of the clergy in marital breakdown situations did not take into consideration the devastating effect and all the upheaval and life change that this situation would have on their children. Most of these young people have lost their faith all together and want nothing to do with God or the church.

They see their mother going through huge social challenges alongside the challenges with clergy and hierarchy, they experience hardship and upheaval, then a number also experience after time seeing less and less of their father. A percentage of clergy do all they can to keep contact with their children but, due to the nature of the clergy persons calling, families of a clergy person know that their calling is also a sacrificial one where the clergy person's time is concerned. Separation and divorce causes some children to have less time with their fathers and situations become more intense. The children need to be a priority in this sad situation and should never be used as an excuse to cause more damage or as a blackmailing tool.

As accounts started to be sent to me, I didn't know how I was going to be able to cope or deal with all the heartbreaking information about the spouses and their children, as I was still going through my own loss and grieving process. The spouses were going through the worst of situations. A number of the clergymen had none or very little understanding and compassion for the dire circumstances they had put their clergy spouses and children in, and the upheaval the abandoned spouse and family were in, with a percentage being left homeless. It is totally unacceptable that homelessness should be the experience of anyone including clergy spouse and children.

The clergy people experience little change in their lives as they still maintain their security in their vicarages and jobs, while a percentage of spouses were having to start again in other family's homes or room surfing or in mostly rented accommodation in a new area, new schools to deal with, without their church family support, as most of the congregations had no idea what was happening to the clergy spouse and children. Congregations are most often not told the truth about the clergy marriage breakdown.

This piece of work is to raise awareness and to bring about change to a very serious problem within the very fabric of the Church of England family of God. In a family situation, if there is a problem and it is not faced correctly and dealt with in a way that is beneficial to all, it becomes a bigger problem. Difficult situations in all walks of life need to be faced, talked about, and brought to a conclusion that is for the well-being of the whole. I hope by the end of this book that's what eventually in practice may in time be accomplished within the church. The wheels of certain institutions sometimes turn slowly, but Broken Rites trying to mend some of the ways a clergy breakdown is handled and not having a satisfactory conclusion since it was formed 35 years ago, is a very serious problem. Many of us over the years have tried to internally sort this serious problem out, but to no avail.

We currently have no power to make a solid change, but we at Broken Rites are going to move forward in every way possible until the establishment hear our voice and help us and the children who are or were part of the Church of England family of God. Many of us have been through hell due to the way the clergy spouse situation is handled in the Church of England. There is a group of very strong men and women in Broken Rites who are going to keep advancing forward towards change, and we are not going to stop - even if it takes the rest of our lives. Our goal and aim is that not one more clergy spouse and family will go through what a number of us have been through these past 35 years and beyond.

Broken Rites AGM 2018

Forward from *The RT Hon Frank Field President*

I understand that differences between denominations and differences between the various Dioceses in the Church of England are becoming more obvious, so that whilst some people receive excellent support, others receive little and feel that their voices are not heard, nor their problems understood. Here I shall work with your committee so that the church responds positively, as I'm sure they will. The practical and pastoral care separated spouses/partners receive, varies according to where they live and which church their spouse belongs to.

I have been concerned to hear that separated spouses/partners of members of the clergy are once again experiencing homelessness or are precariously housed and that fewer are being helped with housing by the churches. Many are in insecure privately rented accommodation with the fear of rent rises and forced moves for the rest of their lives. That this does not need to be so was demonstrated at the 2017 AGM when members heard how the Church of Scotland provides for its members, including housing support and pastoral care.

I support Broken Rites in their call for a UK-wide standard of support for this vulnerable group, and I call upon all churches to make such statistics as they have available to the committee of Broken Rites so that they can plan how best to respond to the needs of separated and divorced spouses/partners of the clergy.

Marriages fail for whatever reasons, but no wife and children should be abandoned and "Set Adrift" without a home, safety and adequate provision. This is all against what God the Father of us all wants for us. If you are in a position of power, reading this with power to make changes, please do something, not just protecting clergy people, but also protecting spouses and children. Many spouses and children lose their faith when going through this situation, this is very serious. We all must take into account eternal perspectives not just temporary perspectives.

Why did Jesus say, "A new commandment I give to you, Love one another"? Were they not loving one another? Throughout this book I'm going to refer back to these following words EL ROI "I AM The God Who Sees You". I say these words for no other reason only that they are true and every one of us need to remember these words in all of our dealings. None of us are perfect and every one of us get it wrong at times, but He sees our motives and hearts and reasons for all of our decisions, and we need to bear that in mind on a daily basis. If something is wrong in our lives, we need to wake up and change it. Sometimes we get comfortable in our situations, we need to get uncomfortable and put ourselves in other people's shoes, then act accordingly.

Unfolding The Rose

(Darryl L Brown)

It is only a tiny rosebud
A flower of God's design
But I can't unfold the petals
With these clumsy hands of mine

The way of unfolding flowers
Is not known to such as I
The flower God opens sweetly
In my hands would surely die

If I can't unfold a rosebud
This flower of God's design
Then how can I have wisdom?
To unfold this life of mine

So I will trust Him to lead me
Each moment of every day
And I'll ask Him to guide me
Each step of the way

For the pathway before me
My Heavenly Father knows
And I'll trust Him to unfold it
Just as He unfolds the rose

Chapter 1

El ROI "I AM THE GOD WHO SEES YOU"

After a lifetime of living comfortably in a safe environment, very quickly I found myself overnight losing my spouse who I loved, my dog who I adored, my home, church family, geographical area, financial security and soon after my job. I lost everything overnight; I had no home or means of providing myself with a home. Two years later I found out my experience was far from unique. The rentals are high and often out of clergy spouses reach until finances are settled which takes time with some accounts of spouses waiting longer than 4 years and up to ten years for the finances to be settled. No one is monitoring this situation in respect of the partner in need. Spouses on little means when divorce proceedings begin do not have the means for a solicitor, so the clergy spouses have to go through the process alone facing their clergy partner's solicitors with all of their experience, as opposed to a clergy spouse having no experience. Clergy spouses have tried to go through mediation, which is a very low-cost way through the divorce system, with a person mediating between the spouse and clergy person. Some clergy would not go through mediation and chose to go through the court system. For many of us, it was the first time in a court building - a daunting experience and a place we thought we would never have to enter.

Unfortunately, some of us have experienced and now understand the real meaning of poverty, in the court waiting areas as we sat in the public areas watching our clergy spouses sitting in private rooms with their legal representatives while we had to represent ourselves. Also, many clergy spouses understand and have experienced the universal credit system, the housing benefit system and in my case as well as others, the difficulty of finding jobs in very deprived areas of the country where many people are applying for every job.

My experience of the Universal Credit system was very distressing. On my first visit a grown man was screaming and crying begging for help for him and his children, he was shouting he had no food. His distress was great. If I'd had any money at the time, I would have given him it. Every time I had to go and sign on, I found it incredibly shattering. I couldn't believe I was now living in, and now part of this world of poverty and completely understanding and experiencing the "Daniel Blake" world and existence. It was a distressing visible reminder of the poverty line I was now on with other clergy spouses going through or who had gone through the same system after their marriage had broken down.

A Message To Clergy Spouses

Clergy spouse, whatever denomination you belong to, whatever country you are living in, this book is for you to help you in your plight, you are not alone. We are here for you Broken Rites UK Contact us and your true support will begin. We have Broken Rites Reps for the UK, Europe and USA. www.brokenrites.org

A Message To Church Members

I want to talk to you now if you are a church member in the Church of England or any denomination, as you read my story you are going to be shocked and saddened. You will not want to believe it but my voice as I've stated is one within a collective group of 150+ clergy spouses. After what has happened to me personally and many others, I cannot walk away from this very serious issue, I wish I could. We at Broken Rites don't want one more clergy spouse to go through what many of us have been through. As stated, even if it takes the rest of our lives, many of us in Broken Rites will work towards bringing in a caring safety net through an adequate "National Care Policy for Clergy Spouses" going through this horrendous plight.

Curious readers' wanting to know what this is all about, I want to assure you of one thing. People are people and we all make mistakes, but be assured, Jesus way is very different from these accounts that many clergy spouses have endured. A number of clergy spouses and their children have gone through an incredible lack of care and compassion. None of this is God's fault. Whenever we go through difficult awful times, many people straight away blame God. When we take the time and learn who God is, He is far from the one at fault when suffering occurs. If we all followed His ways and showed His love and compassion, the world would be transformed. But it takes each one of us as individuals to change. We all have free will, God did not make us like robots to follow Him, He gave us free will and a model of the life and character of Jesus to consider following. Not the words, rules, laws and ways of men and systems but to follow the words, and 2 Golden Rules of Jesus:

1. **To Love God**
2. **To Love Others**

In one sense this whole book could hang on those two golden rules. If every one of us Loved God and Loved Others the way He wants us to, there would be no need for this book. The world would be transformed if we all looked to Jesus and studied His character and followed his ways and his example to all people. He was and is wise and very loving, caring, powerful and strong. But His power doesn't corrupt. His character is beautiful and spotless. He went out of the city to find the lepers who everyone had rejected. He went to a graveyard where some people had chained a man up, He went to bring healing to the lepers and release to the man in the cemetery. He came to set us all free, to change us inside and to fill our hearts with His love. He has compassion on us all and He cares about you and your needs. He leaves the ninety-nine and goes looking for the one who is lost.

Be assured the clergy spouses in Broken Rites have done all we can to be heard internally within the system and continue to do so. Some are hearing our voice, but we are not being cared for the way that we should be through marriage breakdown with all the complexities including the nightmare of tied housing. We have no other option but to do all we can as individuals to raise awareness and try to bring into being a system change towards this very serious issue of there not being an adequate safety net for clergy spouses and their children, when clergy marriages are in trouble.

I am ashamed to write these next few words but I'm going to. Over and over again as I was collating the evidence for this book, I asked the clergy spouses "was anyone happy with the practical support they needed during the time of the marriage breakdown?" Were they provided for in a place of safety if needed? I was asking that question because none of the accounts showed adequate care and support for the clergy spouse and children, so quite a few times I asked that question. The numbers of clergy spouses who said they were adequately provided for was only one, although a few more clergy spouses have recently been added to that number.

This group of 150+ is a very small percentage of clergy marriages in the overall UK percentage 2016 figures of clergy across the UK. But even if one clergy spouse was not cared for and his or her children, that would be one family to many.

In our darkest hour after living our lives supporting others and being part of the church family, the lack of practical support was absent for many of us. This group of women majorities kept silent and spread no malicious words or gossip, we protected church flocks and the very system and men we supported pushed us out of the city gates. Would you push any person out of your church or denomination? No I'm sure you wouldn't. There are of course Bishops, Archdeacons and clergy who are appalled and supportive of the clergy spouse plight and give us hope, but we need change nationally so that all of the hierarchy can hopefully understand that a national approach across the board is what is so needed to rectify this dilemma.

It is not my intent to bring any detriment to an individual person or system. We have done everything in our power to be heard and our very urgent pleas are most often not heard or taking too much time to be heard when action is needed urgently. Some of the hierarchy circle around the clergy person regardless of their conduct, and some of their conduct is appalling and far from the ways of a Holy God who sees everything and knows everything. Some clergy marriages unfortunately do come to an end but when that is the case, especially for a clergy person, they and the system should at least make sure that the spouse and children are safe and provided for - at least temporarily.

Unfortunately we have many accounts of lies being mass spread following marriage breakdown. This brings so much extra pain and grief to the clergy spouse going through so much loss as they then have to also face their reputations being smashed to pieces, to protect the clergy person. A marriage breakdown is enough without the clergy spouse being subjected to an onslaught of rumors, presumptions and lies being spread far and wide.

Regardless of the marriage breakdown this is not the worst of the issues, but how the breakdown is handled and lies is the worst part of the process. Whatever the issue for a marital breakdown as devastating as that is, it can be forgiven. But when shrouded in lies the result is further trust issues occurring which are practically impossible to move on from. Those who admit reasons for marriage breakdowns and deal with the consequences and are sorry, even though there is much for the couple to work through there may be a chance of a marriage survival. But reasons and denial of the truth of a marriage breakdown brought the greatest pain to everyone involved. Clergy marriage breakdown brings great damage not only to the spouse and family but much further afield. There are very damaging consequence to many people.

When so much bad news and lies are spread around, a clergy spouse gets to the point where the lies that are told about them and what people think about them no longer matters. When you have been publicly scrutinized, misunderstood, judged, and presumptions rather than the truth to be sought and considered has "gone out there", you can never get those lies back or put that right, you eventually get to a place where public opinion no longer hurts you. When anyone is highly criticized in the public eye, a person will either sink under the weight of it, or swim. We see this all the time in the media when celebrity's personal lives are constantly lied about in the press. That is one reason I do not buy newspapers or believe what is written in the media. We are all aware of fake news; it has been going on for a long time. The clergy spouses I have met are survivors regardless of the "Fake News".

As a clergy spouse, unfortunately most things that are said about us gets back to us in time. I personally have been deeply hurt by many things that have got back to me. I don't want to know what those who don't know the truth decide, judge and gossip about, but unfortunately that is just a hazard that goes with the territory of a clergy public marriage breakdown. Thankfully the numbers of clergy marriage breakdown are small, but this adds to the increase of public speculation, judgement and presumption, without knowing the facts. Jesus despised the shame of the cross, but he publicly and willingly went to the cross to save us from our sins knowing what was to be accomplished on the cross. We have despised the shame of the marriage breakdown even when that has not been our decision. But raising awareness and working towards change has got to be the good coming out of this shame and injustice. Many people all over the world are crying out for justice against cruel individuals and systems despising the shame of whatever is their issue.

At the beginning of a clergy marital breakdown, it is incredibly painful and embarrassing for the clergy spouse - especially as the statements that go out and are read out to the church congregations are often not true. The accounts have shown that some clergy who end marriages are allowed to write the statement that will be read out to the church. Due to the fact that some clergy write their own statement, this practice is very unfair because it leaves the speculation of why the marriage has ended, which in turn leaves the situation wide open to criticism, which is then directed towards the clergy spouse. We are not an appendage of a clergy person; we are individuals with our own rights. But these rights over and over again are taken from us, at a time of incredible weakness and vulnerability.

The clergy spouse is put under so much pressure by senior staff that they have to go along with the statement going public. A few weeks after I had to leave the vicarage, I was sent a statement already written that was going to be read out to the church. I protested at the speed of the ending to our marriage, but the church leader in charge of the statement process was ploughing through with the legalities. I said everything was going too fast and I needed time to get used to what was happening before the breakdown of the marriage went public. The clergy person dealing with the statement said that the congregation needed to know what was happening as they hadn't seen me for a few weeks and were wondering and speculating what was going on. They needed to know! (If that was true or not, I don't know) What about what I needed at that time? A forced statement out so soon was not what I needed, I was reeling from the shock and speed of it all. Many clergy spouses were subjected to this same procedure.

We had lost all of those major things in one go very fast, and then the system put a statement out publicly which is final. The deanery clergy person dealing with my statement had no compassion on me and believed I should get back to work as soon as possible and put all this behind me, accept it and just get on with my life, working in the same deanery as my husband! He had no comprehension whatsoever of what I was going through. The system had to follow through with their procedures and that's the way it was. The statement said that our marriage had irretrievably broken down. "Irretrievably". In my world nothing was irretrievable in Christ. I was still at the point of thinking the opposite of irretrievable, new start, new beginning, hope, resurrection, reconciliation and forgiveness.

These words were not on the lips of the clergy person who was dealing with me, it was over, and I had to accept and deal with that.

I had never been faced with such cold, hard heartedness in my life. This was the case for many clergy spouses.

I have asked and received many accounts from other clergy spouses on what happened to them when their marriages broke down, and many of the clergy spouses received the same treatment from the senior staff and hierarchy, I have accounts of clergy who ended their marriages and then they were allowed to write the statement that were to be read out to the churches. Statements that completely covered over their reasons for ending their marriages and saying that the clergy spouse had left the vicarage and moved on. The clergy spouse was not only dealing with the grief and reasons of a marriage breakdown and loss of partner, home and everything else, but also the statement left the congregations thinking the clergy spouse had ended the marriage and left the vicar. Many accounts reported this exact situation. When a new clergy spouse joins Broken Rites although we welcome them, our hearts are breaking - as we know what they are going through and what they will have to deal with through this process. Here are a few instances in which a statement was given out to the church of a clergy marriage breakdown and what the truth was behind the scenes.

1) A clergyman came in one day and announced to his wife the reason why he no longer wanted to be married to her. The clergyman then went away and was given a few months paid leave while the spouse had to swiftly move out of the vicarage. She was first told she did not need to speak about this to anyone, but she insisted that the churchwardens were told. They were told and they helped her to move out of the vicarage. Her husband then went on to add even further heartbreaking reasons as to why he wanted their marriage to end. He was then allowed to write the statement to the churches that his marriage had broken down and his wife had moved out of

the vicarage etc. Leaving the wife open to criticism from people who knew nothing only that the vicar had been left on his own.

2) Another clergy spouse was told that her marriage was over and was sent the majority of the moving out details by email and text, no explanation as to why their marriage was over no concrete reason just an email suggesting she had a few months to leave the vicarage. She had to leave the vicarage and she had nowhere to go and no money even for a let. The statement was then given out to the church very quickly saying that the clergy couple's marriage had broken down and the wife had left the vicarage and moved one. Leaving that wife open to criticism and everyone circling the clergy person abandoned by the wife even though he was the person who had ended the marriage, which is most often the case.

John 14:27b

"My peace I give you. I do not give to you as the world gives. Do not let your heart be troubled and do not be afraid".

"Lay your head upon me and cling to me. Draw close enough to hear my heart beating, as I hear yours. Trust that I am with you. Place your grief and sadness at My feet, that I may fill your heart with My peace that passes all understanding. Come, little one, come rest in Me".

Clergy Spouse

Northern Province

I was devastated over what had happened in losing my husband to a parishioner then also having to face the incredible difficulty of my very poor financial situation. I lost my husband to someone else and my home and financial security, this all compounded the grief I was experiencing. The flat I was then offered and moved into I soon became aware that it was across the road from an active drugs dealer with people coming and going at all times of the day and night. I had gone from living in safe homes and safe areas all my life to now being subjected to these living conditions. I had little sleep for years because people would often congregate at the side of my flat after midnight, feet away from my bedroom window. Police cars would often pass or stop with their lights filling my bedroom in the middle of the night. I used to wake up frightened wondering what was going on out there. It was a nightmare at times. I had been subjected to this way of living and blamed for my marriage breakdown by my clergy husband.

Chapter 2

Galatians: The Charter Of Freedom

Broken Rites have a number of clergy spouses that do still, by the Grace of God, have a strong faith in our God who loves and cares for each one of us. He wants the very best for every person, and when things go wrong in our lives and we face great difficulties and storms that come in many guises (ill health, the loss of employment, the loss of loved ones, the loss of homes etc.), God will either bring great good out of our difficulties or He will greatly strengthen us, comfort and help us during those dark times. A percentage of us lost everything overnight when our marriages broke down, but during those difficult times, as we trusted God in such dire circumstances, He brought about too many coincidences that we, as Christian believers, know were God incidences. His care and presence in other ways was always evident.

Moving on to Galatians. The greatest freedom, I believe, is having peace inside; regardless of circumstances, this is true freedom. We can have grief and sadness, but over the years, as we put our full trust in God, He will put within us great peace, which is not subject to our circumstances. Losing my ex-husband (many clergy spouses have said the same about their partners) was the greatest pain in my life that I have ever experienced. My deep grief at that loss went on for quite some time, but I never lost my peace - apart from a few very difficult days through the shock of a few things that happened. Most people going through the pain of a marriage breakdown will admit going through a stage of not wanting to be married any longer, that is a stage that you can pass through if your belief in the marriage and love of the other person is bigger than the pain at that time you're going through. I cannot divide my story from God in the midst of it, nor would I want to. God is In the midst of your pain and regardless of that pain, He has a plan for your life. Throughout circumstances you may find yourself in, please do me one thing: NEVER lose your HOPE and TRUST in God. One day you will realize how much He loves and cares about you. He wants you more than anything in this world, to understand those facts.

There is a deep yearning within each one of us to be free from any kind of oppression. What holds you back from being totally free, is it an addiction? Or are you being oppressed in some way in your workplace, home, school, or college? When these difficulties are sorted out you will be free inside. Our experience says to you: if you are being oppressed in anyway, seek help today. There are many people or organizations that can help you. Do you need counselling? Is your marriage falling apart? If so, don't wait any longer make an appointment to see a counsellor or a trusted friend. Today get onto the road to recovery, why wait any longer what are you waiting for? An oppressor will not change; a bully will not change unless they want to. You can't do anything about another person's behaviour and ways, you can only change yourself. You don't have to stay in that state of oppression any longer, make a move towards freedom in your heart and mind and life. Don't allow one person or a system to hold you ransom in any way, free yourself today. If you are living with a controlling person, you do not need to be controlled any longer, seek help today, build your strength back up and free yourself from that oppression. I must stress I'm not advocating separation or divorce, far from it, but seek counselling and a way through your challenges.

We are seeing daily on our TV screens people all over the world suffering and revolting against oppression over all kinds of things. We are seeing people fleeing countries in search of freedom and peace. Allow the refuge to live among you in freedom and peace. Don't oppress them; befriend them, care for them, and help them. Clergy spouse: please contact us and we will help you. We know these words and our stories are only the tip of the iceberg. Don't be afraid, don't be isolated any longer, there is a big group of clergy spouses here for you to support you, befriend you and help you. Paul in Galatians was the Father of the early Christian Church. The religious leaders of the day were so wrapped up in rules and regulations that they had lost some essential care and loving ways. They were comfortable beyond belief and knew no real reality of true poverty personally. I and many other clergy spouses know and have experienced poverty on the lowest end of the scale by UK standards.

One of my dear friends was going through a time of poverty. Prior to this time he had a good job outside of the church, but he had a definite calling to give that job up as God wanted to take him on another path. He followed God's leading and went through a time of poverty on his journey to plenty in God's work. He is the most caring, loving, good young Christian man that I know. I learned much from him when he was going through his difficult time. He never complained and continued to trust God 100%.

The Lord lay on my heart at that time that whenever I had more than I needed, I had to make sure this Man of God did not go hungry. During his struggle when I was able to, I took him food. He was always very grateful and immediately, whatever food I had taken him, he shared it into a few piles and gave the other away to other needy people in his street. Every night he would cook dinner and invite people - including very poor people - around his table, and very often some people who no one else invited. After a lifetime of plenty I observed his giving heart. I too had always had that generosity to others, but this was on a different level. My friend travelled through that time of poverty with a gracious trusting spirit. He was an inspiration and continues to be. God has enabled me during my darkest times of poverty to travel through with that same spirit. A great lesson I learned from my new African friends that this friend introduced me to, was when one had no food someone would share the little they had with that friend, and their hospitality even with the little they had, was always given to others. When Paul in Galatians laid the foundations for Christian liberty, he reminded the church that we were saved by faith not by keeping the law. That freedom we have in Jesus means that we are free to love and serve one another. Not to do wrong but to carry each other's burdens and to be kind to each other.

We see as we read Galatians that there was a conflict between grace and the law, faith and deeds. We are free in Jesus but unfortunately some people who see great wrong done to others, are bound by words and laws. A great injustice has been done to many in our group at Broken Rites; certain clergy were not happy with how we were being treated but they had to be silent and retreat away from us. Some clergy spouses were ignored and not helped when they became homeless. Our immediate church family were not able to support us, as they did not know we were in need, but God provided others to help us. I was very blessed to have family and close friends around me who travelled that path with me, praying for me every day. A Bishop, as a gesture of the diocese ongoing support, sent one clergy spouse £500. She was homeless. She received no further help.

When we found Broken Rites; we then realized that the lack of care and help given by our former partners and the senior staff was widespread across the Church of England in the UK. Some clergy husbands and diocese are very helpful and, for this, on behalf of Broken Rites we truly thank you and are very grateful for your love, care and support during this very difficult transitional time. We also know now that if some of us had of been in other diocese, the support needed would have been available. This help should be across the board in every diocese. That is why we are asking if the care policy can be looked at and hopefully changed.

Those dioceses that do not help us, accounts showed that the clergy spouse also had to deal with coldness and hard heartedness. It's a big thing getting in touch with Bishops and senior staff and to be ignored or closed down or to be subjected to a lack of practical love is devastating. God allowed Pharaoh's heart to be hardened to the few men who were approaching him and asking for change. They wanted change so that all the other people would be freed from the cruel regime they were experiencing. We know that others are going to tread the path that we have trod or are on at the moment, and for those of us who are trying to make a change - especially over the way some of the clergy husbands deal with the sharing of assets etc. They should not be allowed to barter with us over percentages of assets and pensions. But those unable to afford legal representation, are at their partner's solicitors' mercy. Which in reality is "no mercy". Everything should be shared equally and fairly. We need help at times along this journey.

Going back to Moses and Aaron, eventually the Israelite slaves were set free and Pharaoh and his great army lost their hold over the Israelites. God set the oppressed free. I write this book so that others will be free in the future from the weight, oppression and abuse that many at Broken Rites have had to face and cope with.

It is our hope as you read this book that you too will be set free from your oppression if need be. Keep your heart soft regardless of what you may face and go through, and always have a heart for others and everyone. As stated, Jesus left us two Royal Rules, only two rules. Love God and Love Others. Were these clergy wives shown love and care, as they were "Set Adrift" with no safety net? We were the person on the other side of the clergy person, yet we have been treated worse than any other person in the church or who comes through the church doors. Where were our shepherds during our darkest hour? Where were they? God sent us other shepherds to help us. Church, no one should be put on a pedestal - everyone should be treated fairly and with respect.

The disrespect that is shown to an ex clergy spouse is appalling. Once clergy friends and church colleagues and friends, now many show disrespect to us and they don't even know our stories. The church naturally side with the priest. We must show respect to all and especially our leaders. I am not being disrespectful by writing this book; I am standing up against a great injustice that has happened to many clergy spouses. We at Broken Rites can't walk away from this, I wish I could, and just get on with my life in a quiet corner of the world. But we can't sit back knowing a great injustice is going on and will continue to go on if we don't do something about it. My words may just drift away and be ignored, or they may be listened to and may help in bringing about change for future clergy spouses.

No one dares to speak of the full injustice; but we cannot keep silent any longer, so I do this for change to protect others whose marriage breakdown will unfortunately happen too. Broken Rites are working away towards change but that change will happen at the church convenience and in the church's time. The wheels turn very slowly in the Church of England but can speed up at times of serious issues that need addressing urgently. This lack of safety net for clergy spouses and their children is an urgent issue that needs immediate attention. 35 years Broken Rites have been working towards change, 35 years! Our hearts break for all the new clergy spouses that join our group at Broken Rites because we know what they will learn as the years pass. We know of the hurt and frustration and further abandonment they will suffer at the hands of the church leadership.

A Message To Archbishop Justin Welby

I and we at Broken Rites believe that Archbishop Justin Welby is a man of great integrity and a man striving for change and justice for all in and outside of the church. He wants to eradicate homelessness; he wants to revise the Universal Credit System, which I who have experienced it, totally agree with. It is a cruel hard-hearted system that drives some people already on the poverty line, to the brink of suicide. People on Universal Credit included people like me, and many who have worked all or most of their lives but then have had a very unexpected turn of events for the worst. I never thought in a million years that I would ever be on the poverty line and on Universal Credit.

It was a shocking experience, so shocking for me, the pressure this system caused me was so intense that one day I walked out of the Universal Credit building after telling the person who was dealing with me that I didn't want their help any longer. I walked away with nothing, not a penny to my name, and I didn't know what I was going to do. I was trying desperately to find another job. I went self-employed and started again with not one penny. The Universal Credit system was making it impossible for me to move forward in my business and putting further pressures on me that were impossible to fulfil. The way I used to feel when in that building listening to what they were saying to me was often quite devastating.

My existence was dire and the pressure the Universal Credit System put on me was too much to handle at times. The people who work there are just doing their job; but the rules at times are not at all helpful for individuals trying to set up self-employed. The rules work against you and are not helpful.

I felt as though I was in a living nightmare. One day as I listened to the lady telling me how to run my work life and business I thought if I don't get out of here now, I would end up at the mercy of this system. So I walked away into nothing - no funding from anywhere, just me on my own. As I walked away from Universal Credit that day, the pressure lifted, and I felt free even though I didn't know how I was going to survive. I very soon found out that as a self-employed person I was allowed Tax Credits of £52 a week (that is $66) while building my business. That was exactly the same money I had walked away from under the Universal Credit System, which was my only weekly income at that time. Now I was getting the same money, but it was just paid into my bank every week and no more signing on and following Universal Credit System rules. I'd made a huge step forward. Nearly 200 job applications later I secured a part-time post after my brother-in-law advised me to leave my date of birth off my CV/Resume, I secured the very next post I applied for. Going back to Archbishop Justin, we believe if he knew properly of the plight of clergy spouses and their children, he would help us. We are trying to reach him with the urgency for change in the plight of the clergy spouse and children. He does not hide things under the carpet - he faces the most awful issues and deals with them and to him, this group of his wider flock in Broken Rites reaches out for an adequate "National Care Policy".

The clergy spouses need a safety net and especially where the tied housing is concerned. A percentage of us lose our safety, security and home when our marriages breakdown. I have personally been in some very unsafe places since losing my home. One night in the place I had to stay, I sat up all night fully clothed waiting for the daylight to come so I could move on. I could hear police car sirens all night long; I was very afraid and prayed all night for safety and the protection of God over me. I will expand on my living options when I lost my home in the next chapter.

Throne Room Lyrics

Kim Walker-Smith

Dream after dream You are speaking to me,
Breathing Word after word of Kingdom come
Here at your feet I can see the unseen
Truly One look at you and I'm undone
I run to the throne room I run to the throne room
And I fall on my face with angels and saints and all I can say is
Holy, holy, holy are You, God
My heart can't contain the weight of Your name and all I can say Is,
Holy, holy, holy are You

Grace upon grace all my fear falls away only
Your perfect love for me remains Oh,
time after time you stay close by my side burning
Fire inside I can't contain

I run to the throne room I run to the throne room
And I fall on my face with angels and saints and all I can say is
Holy, holy, holy are You, God
My heart can't contain the weight of Your name and all I can say Is,
Holy, holy, holy are You

I run to the throne room Before You, the only One
I run to the throne room Before You, I'm overcome
I run to the throne room Before You, the only One
I run to the throne room Before You, I'm overcome

And I fall on my face with angels and saints and all I can say is
Holy, holy, holy are You, God
My heart can't contain the weight of your name and all I can say Is,
Holy, holy, holy are you

Chapter 3

Jimmy Wayne "Walk To Beautiful"

During my first year without my own home, I room surfed staying in 5 people's homes. My close friends gave me keys to their front doors, I stayed in 3 of those homes when they went on holidays, another home I stayed at random times throughout that first year - another couple's home I visited many times. Another home I was so deep in grief, it was so difficult just existing through this period.

For the first two and a half years I had countless meals in my car, a local supermarket did a substantial salad for £2.49 - I didn't want to put on people. I used to drive to the beach and spent many hours there. I also drove up to the Cathedral which had been a part of my life for many years and which I'd had the privilege of planning with a team and leading music in 5 summer children's services for quite a few years.

The grief of not being part of the church overwhelmed me many times. I sat outside the Cathedral so many times till very late on a night. I was lost, without a home of my own and I had lost my church family and denomination. I didn't know where I belonged anymore. I would drive past thousands of homes day after day begging God to give me a home again. I just wanted a place I could be at rest in and call "my home" again. It may not be possible for me to ever have my own home again as I don't have enough years of mortgage time left to me now. I was rootless and so desperate to have a home again. My parents are elderly, so I hardly shared anything of my daily struggles with them - I didn't want to bring such trouble to their door or worry them. I was in such a fog that first year after I had to leave "my home/ vicarage" etc that I went to see my doctor once because I felt so ill; he told me I was going through a grieving process. Praying became impossible for me, after a lifetime of prayer, so all I prayed for that first year most of the time quietly in my mind was "Jesus, please help me" that's all I could say.

I couldn't listen to the radio anymore as much as I loved music because most songs reminded me of my ex-husband, but I loved Daryl's House on YouTube, he had great guests on, and their musicianship was excellent.

I listened to artists I hadn't heard of before and songs that had no connection with my past. I listened to my favourite songs on there, one of them was "Sara Smile" - Jimmy Wayne's Version. I had never heard of him until I came across him on Daryl's House. I loved his version and his creativity with that classic song and how he made it his own. It was instantly my most favourite version of that song.

I didn't Google Jimmy Wayne or listen to any of his other songs for quite a while. I just went back to Daryl's House Channel on YouTube and listened a few times to my favourites. The songs and excellent musicianship made me feel happy inside. I then came across Jimmy Wayne's book "Walk To Beautiful" - I couldn't believe the content. His mother abandoned Jimmy at a young age, just before he was a teenager. The way he described that abandonment from his perspective then as a young person, resonated within me about my experience. It was the first writing I had come across and person who described exactly how I was feeling inside. Jimmy was just a kid when he lost everything, how he survived I don't know, but I thought if a kid survived, then I could survive.

His real-life story was a lifeline for me, and an inspiration at that time in my life. His story gave me hope to keep on going even when I felt so weary by the sheer struggle I was going through. At every turn, everyday my life had turned into this massive struggle, life itself was overwhelming, and I sometimes felt like I didn't have the strength to carry on. But that little kid Jimmy kept going and now as an adult God was using him in a mighty way to help thousands of foster kids. Read his book, Jimmy's story and his life now is a huge inspiration. I gleaned so much strength from his story. There were parts of Jimmy's book that at that time I couldn't read, I was too broken, but his story was the only thing that came close to an understanding of what I was experiencing at that time (this was before I was told about broken rites, so still at a stage where I felt very alone in my experience). Thank you, Jimmy, for writing "Walk To Beautiful" and continued blessings on all the incredible work you and Jacquelyn are doing. You are both an inspiration.

While researching into clergy marriage breakdown, I found a piece of work that was completed in Australia. It showed shocking statistics, 93% of clergy wives lost their faith in God and also stopped going to church as they were abandoned by the very system that they had given their lives to. I was so shocked and saddened. That statistic must break God's heart.

I was talking to a clergy friend one day in another diocese and he asked, "Have you been in touch with Broken Rites?" That day I contacted them and I'm so glad I did, they have been a Godsend ever since. That was two years into my plight. I didn't know up until that point of another clergy spouse going through or had gone through a clergy marriage breakdown/separation ending in divorce, I felt totally alone on this journey until that day when I was told about Broken Rites. I went to their website, I wrote to them then suddenly I'm part of a large group of spouses who understood fully what I was going through. I could breathe again, they showed me a deep level of care, understanding, support and love. I shared my deep grief with them, they took hold of my hands and enabled me to get on my feet again, they completely understood my pain because they had all experienced the same path I was on. My friends and family prior to this had been so important to me and now Broken Rites. Clergy spouse, if you need us, we are here for you. Contact us at www.brokenrites.org

At this point I just want to say: my ex-husband knew none of what I was going through, we had no communication from early on in the separation period. It is my hope that he will be left in peace to carry on with his life.

He Knows

Jeremy Camp

All the bitter weary ways
Endless striving day by day
You barely have the strength to pray
In the valley low
And how hard your fight has been
How deep the pain within
Wounds that no one else has seen

Hurts too much to show
All the doubt you're standing in between
And all the weight that brings you to your knees

He knows He knows
Every hurt and every sting
He has walked the suffering
He knows He knows
Let your burdens come undone
Lift your eyes up to the one who knows

We may faint and we may sink
Feel the pain and near the brink
But the dark begins to shrink
When you find the one who knows
The chains of doubt that held you in between
One by one are starting to break free

He knows He knows
Every hurt and every sting
He has walked the suffering
He knows He knows
Every hurt and every sting He has walked the suffering
He knows He knows
Let your burdens come undone
Lift your eyes up to the one who knows

Chapter 4

Cliff Richard Trauma To The Soul

As already stated, some clergy spouse's assets take from a few years up to ten years to be released. Until the finances are resolved, the clergy spouse is in unsettled living arrangements. This interim stage is such a difficult and uncertain place to be long-term. It's a very unsettling place. Until finances are resolved, the clergy spouse is at the mercy of a very difficult existence. That being just one issue - the lack of a home and tied-housing is the most important issue that needs to be resolved.

As I read the accounts and true-life experience of other clergy spouses the tears were flowing. Many of the issues are hard to even put into words - what some of the women have had to deal with is indescribable. I also received details from a male spouse as he poured his story out to me including all areas of loss in his life. Every area of his life was turned upside down. As I've said, I have written this book and purposely tried to keep it as factual as possible and mostly kept the emotional sides of our stories at bay.

Even though this is chapter 4 I'm actually writing this chapter near the end of my time writing this whole book and I remain conscious not to stray from the central message. The accounts and information for this book have been taken from clergy spouses experiences from England, Ireland, Scotland and Wales. I'm very happy and pleased to share that favourable reports have come from Scotland.

We have seen in the media recently that Cliff Richard's case has been resolved (not fully, there is more to come, but I recently watched the first interview he gave after he was cleared). Many things he said about his invasion of privacy and the sheer lies that have gone out publicly, that he can never wipe away from people's memories. His interview struck many chords with the clergy spouse group. We understand through experience some of his pain. He said for the past few years he has only been able to sleep for two hours per night due to the ordeal he has been going through. The reason he has not been able to sleep correctly for so long is that he has been going through a trauma of the soul. The invasion into his life to this degree has affected his very core in a way that he has never experienced before. Hell was let loose on his life and has devastated much of it.

We read about a similar story in the bible about a man called Job. He had everything that is precious in life; he had a family, a wife, children, sons and daughters. Lavish properties, servants, much livestock and wealth. He had it all, "living the dream" people would say in this day and age. God allowed great loss to come into Job's life. Through a certain set of circumstances, Job lost everything: his children, possessions, staff and servants (who I'm sure would have been his close friends). His wife was spared. On top of all of that loss, Job also lost his health. As Job's wife and friends looked on, they accused Job of many things, and made his life even more painful than it was. Job was actually alone with not one friend standing by his side. Job was a righteous man; in his agony of soul he asked God questions. If you have never done so, please read the book of Job for yourself; his life has much to teach us.

God answered Job's questions in a remarkable way. God reprimanded Job's friends because they had judged Job in a wrong way. They did not know Job's heart and motives before God, but God knew. He knew everything about Job, and He loved him with an unconditional love. In His love God restored everything and more back to Job.

God will also restore in His way, much back to Cliff Richard and He will restore much back to you if you have encountered great loss in your life. Do not blame God for your loss but know that He is a friend who sticks closer than a brother and knows the real you. He knows your heart and your motives, and He loves you with an everlasting love. His love for you is permanent and secure, and He will NEVER leave you or forsake you even when others do. He will always be right there with you comforting and helping you through your "Dark night of the soul". He will restore to you all you have lost and more. My dear friend Jackie always says, "He will give you double for your trouble".

Going back to Sir Cliff's story about his lack of sleep, many clergy spouses and I know and understand that depth of trauma. A number of clergy spouses are not through the trauma yet; sleep patterns have not been restored, as we've had to live through great trauma to the soul.

When you lose your spouse in the way we at Broken Rites have, we were not allowed a normal grieving process. We were ushered away undercover keeping everything as quiet as possible. Many of us were told by the establishment to "just move on" in our lives and were wished well in our "new life" by senior staff. Moving on under a cloud of secrecy. No Mercy move on after two, three or four decades of married life and security, and building homes; some of us lost all of that, and we are told to just move on. We encountered a tsunami of the soul. Everything in one fell swoop was washed away. Everything that was familiar was gone; I can't even begin to explain how devastating that was. So devastating that this book has been birthed because we don't want one more clergy spouse to experience such devastation without a proper care package in place. I thank God for "Broken Rites" who show unconditional love to all. Together we are facing the facts of the clergy spouse situation, and together we will do everything in our power to bring about permanent change to protect future clergy spouses' and their children.

Clergy Spouse

Southern Province

As the Bishop has dismissed my complaint through the CDM, (Clergy Disciplinary Measures) about my ex-husband's adultery, amongst other things I hired a private investigator that has carried out covert surveillance and written a report of his findings, with photographs that prove beyond doubt that the affair is still ongoing. My solicitor sent this report, along with witness statements to the Deputy President of Tribunals at the legal office in London. We had a reply, which said that the Bishop had made his determination, I had no right of appeal and there is no way I can legally present new evidence. It also said that discipline is a matter for the Bishop only and there is no action the Deputy President can take. So today I took the file along to the archdeacon who was very reluctant to have anything to do with it but said he would send it to the legal office. I told him they already had the file and have said it is not their concern. The Archdeacon then said he would send the file to the Bishop but then added that the

Bishop would send it to the legal office. Does anybody know what I should do with this new evidence? I am very tempted right now to phone the Telegraph and tell them to get round to the vicarage where they will be able to observe the vicar leave in his car, drive to his lovers house and pick her up, taking her back to the vicarage where he will remain with her 6-9 hours before returning her to her home and to her husband around midnight. (Used with Permission)

Situation after situation is presented but to no avail. We at Broken Rites are not under any illusions here as to how the system works. I can actually see in the whole scheme of the official complaints, why complaints of this nature are not dealt with in the way we at Broken Rites believe they should be.

"The CDM "constitutes a complete legal structure but all of it is managed within the institution of the church". At the heart of the system is the Bishop of the diocese. He has the power to declare a case of complaint to be of insufficient interest or substance to take further. Much evidence is presented in many cases and then deemed as insufficient. Even when the complaint is taken to the next stage the Bishop still has the power to take no further action. It is only with the Bishop's consent that the most serious cases come to a tribunal for assessment. Making a diocesan Bishop into a judge and jury over some difficult and intractable situations of misbehaviour of clergy would seem impossible. How can the chief pastor of the diocese successfully or easily fulfil this role? Their role is one of simultaneously caring and judging".

(Survivingchurch.com)

Being totally realistic through the facts I have received and my own personal experience, the clergy are cared for and the clergy spouse is judged by many. The church has created a self-contained legal structure for itself. I could go deep into this but I'm not going to. This picture is very easy to understand. In my simple logic this system is impossible, the costs are huge both financially for the church and emotionally for all concerned. Months in the waiting for results causing unbearable strain for all concerned, knowing at the end of the day the Bishop has the final word. Broken Rites members/ clergy spouses are on the losing end to start with and predominantly are placed in that position by basically a complaints system that is completely unfair. There needs to be an independent body dealing with complaints that have destroyed people's lives. The clergy know how the system works they have assurance from their Bishop that he/ she will support them because in first light of situations the Bishops have to believe the clergy person and their account. The clergy are in a bad stage of their lives anyway when covering up situations to protect themselves, they have no just and fair boundaries in place over the way they will deal with the soon to be ex-wife/husband; giving them free reign to treat the clergy spouse very badly. This is fact from account after account; this behaviour is a common thread throughout the accounts.

Chapter 5

Bob Farrell "I Will Be"

"The day of reckoning refers to the Last Judgment of God in Christian belief, during which time everyone after death is called to account for their actions committed in life". That explanation I'm sure speaks to every one of us about our actions and our motives. Be assured, I'm not pointing the finger here because as we point at others three fingers are pointing back at us. "All have sinned and fallen short of the glory of God"

I wrote a letter to the Bishops here in my diocese, and senior staff, but didn't send it for quite a while. I was afraid of further rejection, which I knew many clergy spouses had been subjected to as well, so I was holding back. My few attempts for help had not been dealt with, as was a common occurrence for many clergy spouses across the UK. Recently I decided to read a book I chose one book I had started to read a little while ago, a book titled "I Will Be" by Bob Farrell.

Bob is an author and also very successful in the field of music that God had called him too, but unfortunately, he took on a business partner who he really trusted, and the business partner ended up getting Bob into a situation where he had to go bankrupt. He ended up living in a condo and the shock of what had happened to him closed him down emotionally for a year. Bob said he sat in a chair in the living room for a year; he couldn't share his pain with those closest to him, not even his wife.

He eventually came to a point where he started opening up again and allowing others to help him out of the difficulty, he was in. He realised fear of certain issues had paralyzed him from moving forward.

While I was reading his book, I had to be honest with myself and recognise two areas in my life, one area I had closed down in was through the fear of being rejected by the hierarchy of the Church of England in my diocese. The email I wrote to them I was sharing my heart with them and that took a lot of courage, and to risk having that rejected? I didn't know if I was strong enough to handle that. But I knew this time I had to face this issue and another issue. Bob encouraged the reader to share and be honest about areas you needed help in. So, I told a few people close to me, those areas I needed support in. It was helpful to vocalize those areas and to hear myself admit these limitations in order to be able to face them head on and sort them out.

Last night I listened to a live video of an amazing prayer warrior and mighty Man of God Marcus Rodgers from the USA. He is on fire for Jesus, truth and holiness in life, and he was saying you are steps away from the Promised Land, but you've got to face that thing that is holding you back so that you can be free and take those last few steps to the Promised Land. As soon as his live broadcast was finished (about 10 minutes long), I went straight to the email and read it a few times. I wanted to post it there and then, but it was late, so I decided to leave it until first thing the next morning. However, I was still awake at 4am thinking it all over I couldn't sleep, and I had a very important meeting at 10am - I needed to sleep. So I got up and went to my computer and added a sentence explaining my reason as I have just done here for posting the email so early in the morning. I prayed for God's help after I finally had emailed it out to my Bishops and senior staff. I still didn't go to sleep for a few hours after that, but I knew something had changed in me, regardless of their response, I felt relief and a freedom I hadn't felt before.

When I had first started reading Bob's book "I Will Be" his loss was so great and the reaction of shock to his body in dealing with the dishonesty and betrayal of his business partner was so great, I could feel the shock as I read his book and I couldn't read past that section for a while until I felt stronger. When I finally had the strength to continue reading and put into practice the few areas I was afraid of facing, once I had shared those areas with my sister and a few others I was able to move forward. What I learned from moving forward in the area of the possibility of further rejection, was from that moment on as I sent that email, I lost the fear of what anyone thought about me or said about me. This is an area that many of us at Broken Rites have had to face, rejection and a huge lack of love, care and compassion from those we thought would never treat us so coldly.

You may be stuck in life in certain areas and if you are, take Bob's advice and share those road blocks and obstacles that are holding you back, talk to a few people who you love and trust. Be perfectly honest with them, don't hold back. Your release and breakthrough may be only one conversation away. When we have great loss and heartbreak in life, we are very vulnerable broken people until we become strong again. In that brokenness we must trust a few people close to us who will help and protect us. I am praying for you, it is my pray that whoever reads these words will be set free and move on to greater inner strength and healing.

Isaiah 43:19

"Behold I will do a new thing; now it shall spring forth".

If God says He's going to bless you, ignore your circumstances and believe God who cannot lie. You're too important to Him to be destroyed by a situation designed to build character and give you direction. God's grace will enable you to make it through. "God proved that He could bring you out of the fire without even the smell of smoke, and out of the lion's den without so much as a bite mark. If you want to know what God can do, look at what He's already done for you, and start praising Him".

And that's not all Listen:
Isaiah 43:19

"Behold I will do a new thing; now it shall spring forth." After feeling like you've waited forever, God will suddenly move, and if you're not ready, you'll miss Him.

When the church was born, we read: "Suddenly there came a sound from heaven as of a rushing mighty wind, and it filled all the house where they were sitting" (Acts 2:2) When God decided to bring Paul and Silas out of prison, we read: "And suddenly there was a great earthquake, and immediately all the doors were opened" (Acts 16:26) Are you ready for God to move suddenly? Are you ready for doors to open?

THE WORD TO YOU TODAY IS "I WILL DO A NEW THING: NOW IT SHALL SPRING FORTH." I KNOW THE LORD IS SAYING THIS TO YOU AND ME TODAY.

My African Pastor Jordan and his beautiful wife Eve have supported me 100% since the beginning of this ordeal. They have prayed for me, prayed with me, encouraged me and helped me practically. They made sure I had enough money to get to church every Sunday when I needed help. I hadn't been able to go to church for a while because I didn't have spare money to get there. Pastor Jordan asked me why I hadn't been coming to church, I was very embarrassed to tell him the reason, but God prompted me in my spirit to share my difficulties. When I told pastor Jordan he acted straight away, and from that weekend, every Saturday night until I didn't need this help any longer, Pastor Jordan deposited £10 into my bank account to make sure I got to church on a Sunday. He sent me this message:

"Woman of God, thank you for sharing this and letting me know. We are praying for you. Like I have always said, your story hits at the core of the Anglican establishment. My feelings are that there will be some resistance and they may try to block you in whatever way they can. We are praying that these issues will be brought to light and no one else suffers the way you have. You may find you're not the only person and many other people may come out of the woodwork, so it is also that backlash we are also praying over. We thank God for using you as a voice for the voiceless. In your humility may the Light of Christ that dwells so richly inside of you, shine so brightly. May your actions and your story point those that see and hear to the true Lord Jesus Christ and his ways for us all. You have our blessing and support; you're always in our prayers".

That prayer was sent to me nearly two years prior to me knowing anything about the Broken Rites organisation.

I will speak out

Heartbeat
I will speak out for those who have no voices
I will stand up for the rights of all the oppressed
I will speak truth and justice
I'll defend the poor and the needy
I will lift up the weak in Jesus' name.

I will speak out for those who have no choices
I will cry out for those who live without love
I will show God's compassion
To the crushed and broken in spirit
I will lift up the weak in Jesus name

Imagine the rejection of men can be "the Lord's doing" He'll take what is painful and make it "marvelous in our eyes" You might well see that the worst possible thing that you thought could have happened to you and has happened to you, was the Lord allowing it, and it will suddenly look marvelous in your eyes. He sends no bad, but He allows some things to happen to us for the greater good of many.

Chapter 6

Where is my home?

I know without a doubt that this is going to be one of the most difficult chapters to write as my memory begins to scan through the many pictures, situations and places I have stayed at, been to and experienced these past four years. Four years, two months since I had to leave the vicarage and I still don't have the answer to the title heading of this chapter "Where is my home?" As already stated, It has taken many clergy spouses years to retrieve their financial assets - some up to 10 years while the clergy continue in their posts and vicarages with no pressure of change. For a clergy spouse and children a percentage are "Set Adrift" with no home and little or no finances to set them up in another property long term. The mortgage market is out of reach in today's climate for a number of clergy spouses, and due to their ages they don't have enough years ahead of them for a mortgage.

There is so much running through my mind as I try to gather my thoughts for this part of the book. My eyes are already filling with tears as I see the pictures and remember how I was feeling going through this rootless, homeless experience. While living around different homes the two housing agencies I approached both put me to the top of their housing lists when they heard my story, as I was classed as homeless.

A few days ago, two of my wonderful friends sent me some audio messages telling me how much they loved me and plans for me moving to a wing of their home. Their sincere love and care for me in such a sea of uncertainty has been an anchor bobbing around in the sea on the horizon of my existence these past four years. Their home is a place of refuge, calm, safety, peace and happiness.

My friend at the beginning of these four years when I was feeling totally lost and crushed got hold of me one day and held me for quite a while.

The feeling as she held me was reminiscent of my mother holding me as a child and feeling those fleeting moments of pure love and security, a place of warmth and security and an action that you never wanted to end. As my friend held me she whispered, "let me be your soft place, let our home be your soft pillow". As she said those words, I pictured their home as a soft pillow to lay my head, a place of security; warmth and love just like the closeness of my mother when I was a child in her arms. Not knowing at that time what the future would hold, and how those words would resonate in my spirit and maybe one day become a reality.

The night I had to leave the vicarage I actually felt like I was going to die. I had only felt like that once before in my lifetime, one day 30 years earlier due to an illness that I had, and now thirty years on here was that feeling again. All I wanted at that moment was for everything to be all right again and back to normal before the marital breakdown started to occur. When going through marital breakdown it's so awful and confusing, you go through a range of feelings, at times wanting to be a million miles away to wanting everything to be okay. There are many reasons why relationships break down but there is one reason that we have learned at Broken Rites that marks the end of a relationship, and that is when someone tells you they don't love you anymore, it's over. You can't talk someone out of that statement you have to accept it. If someone says that to you, don't beg him or her, don't lower yourself; you are worth so much more than that. You should be celebrated not just tolerated.

I want to cover a serious situation that you must recognise if you are being subjected to this from another person. It may be a partner, a work colleague, or family member. There is a big difference between sin and evil. The bible clearly states that every one of us have sinned and fallen short of the glory of God. Evil is far removed from sin, evil tries to destroy people. Those who plan to hurt and destroy others have moved far away from sin into the realm of evil. If a person is trying to destroy you, destroy your peace, your reputation, telling lies about you and saying all kinds of evil against you, don't be blind. That is a person that does not love or care about you at all. Protect yourself and your children from such a person.

Jesus and His character are a world apart from sin and evil. Jesus' character and ways are the very opposite of evil. If you have ever nearly been destroyed by a person or company, remember they can never destroy your character. Your character is the real you. Words, rumors, lies, presumptions will hurt you, and for a time quite badly until you learn to rise above this evil.

You do not need anyone's approval; the only approval that counts for anything at the end of the day is God's approval. God looks at your heart and your motives; He looks at the real you. If your reputation has been destroyed by lies, let it go. Get off the road of pain, lies and destructive words towards you, leave that life behind. Turn your back on it, put great distance between you and that evil bus, let it drive further and further away. Get on your bus, your life, your new beginning this day, and drive far away from the past. If you have been tarnished to this degree you will have to make a conscious effort to get on to your bus and make a good life for yourself. Forgiveness is a very important element here. Whenever we wrong another person or they wrong you, forgiving the offence is so crucial to your wellbeing. If you don't forgive and you pursue in order to damage someone further, that is evil. "Forgive us our sins as we forgive those who sin against us" (The Lord's Prayer). Unforgiveness is like a cancer; it will eat you up inside and take away your peace. Let the offence go. Many clergy spouses have suffered injustice, because regardless of what the clergy person has said or done, the hierarchy and senior staff band around the clergy person. These are not my words or opinions, these are gleaned from the research of many clergy spouse's first-hand experiences. With the greatest of respect I say the following because it is true, and it has to be addressed. Unfortunately, it feels as if at times we are dealing with pockets in the church of an OLD BOYS CLUB. In all of our individual dealings with every individual person who crosses our path day by day, if we profess to be a Christian "Christ follower" we need to deal with everyone as Jesus would. The family of God and the whole church is GOD'S CLUB NOT AN OLD BOYS CLUB. Clergy spouses and their children should be dealt with in the light of Christ day by day, until a good conclusion is reached for all concerned, NOT just the clergy person.

As I write this book, it has become very clear that the way the clergy treat a spouse on marital breakdown, has a profound effect on children and teenagers who are part of this sorry mess. To date, the information from all the accounts and through my general dealings and conversations with clergy spouses, not many of these children and teenagers (and some adults now) have a faith in God, nor do they attend church anymore. What they saw their mothers go through at the hands of the clergy person and church has had a very detrimental effect on most of them. These little ones have been badly hurt, that is the truth of the situation; it is very serious in the light of the Word of God. I am a woman of a simple but great faith in the infallible Word of God. My theology is simple, I believe in a God who loves us all regardless of sin and evil. God is bigger than all of that; He loves every one of us with a love inexpressible. We can't earn His love, we just have it, if we want it. His love is eternal for you and for me. He wants us to understand that, and reach out to Him in prayer and thank Him for His love.

He wants us to love and care for each other in that way. When we sin we hide from God, or we hide from others who we know are close to God. We hide, we avoid, but even in all of that God still loves us. Nothing you can ever do will make Him love you any less or any more than He already does right now. Nothing will change that love He has for you. But His heart breaks when we do not love or care for the good of others.

I was very fortunate to be brought up by a father with a great work ethic and a mother who exudes the love of God. Everyone who knows her and has known her will vouch for my words. She is an absolute angel. I had the privilege of watching her pray and read her bible every day for half an hour. As a child I sat with her and watched her devotion to God. Her counsel always to her children was of such love at every turn and situation. She didn't judge others, she wasn't suspicious of others, all she did was love others with such a kind love. Day after day when I learned to drive, I took her to people in need, we went into some dark places and situations at times, we went into places where people were the neediest that I had ever seen before. She went to many people with love, encouragement, prayers and practical actions when needed. She is my role model; she exudes a character full of love. My dad has great compassion for those in need and displays much love in action.

Jesus had compassion on the crowd; He has such love far greater than any one of us. He said, "Father, may they be one as you and I are one. May they also be in us so that the world may believe that you have sent me. I have given them the glory that you gave Me, that they might be one as we are one, I in them and you in Me, so that they may be brought to complete unity. Then the world will know that You sent Me and have loved them even as you have loved Me. Righteous Father, though the world does not know you, I know You and they know that You have sent Me. I have made You known to them and will continue to make You known in order that the love you have for Me may be in them, and that I myself may be in them". (John 17)

Back to the night I had to leave my home, the vicarage. Before I left, I held on to my precious little dog, knowing I couldn't take him with me as I didn't know where I was going to go. He was better off in his familiar home. I wanted to take him with me, but he was old, and I didn't want his life to be turbulent in anyway. He had his bed, toys, security, warmth and home, how could I take him out of that into nothing. Everything in my being wanted to take him with me, but I had to do the best for him that night, it utterly broke my heart.

Thoughts and pictures of our closeness and love played through my mind. I saw him against the cupboard and my legs as I did the washing up each day, I saw him with his little head on my legs as I watched TV. I remembered his walks as God had taught me that this was his time and a little window in his day to explore the world around him, I had learned to never rush him when he stopped many times to smell his surrounds and to explore little nooks and crannies. I saw him one Christmas as he had got me up during the night one night a few days before Christmas day, as he wanted to go downstairs. I followed him and said, "show me what you want" as I always used to say to him when I knew he wanted to take me to something. This night he stood at the sitting room door, so I opened the door for him, he wandered in and went straight to his bag of doggie Christmas presents and stuck his head straight into his bag, then threw up in the air out of the bag one of his Christmas presents.

I held him closer as these memories filled my mind, I buried my face in his fur as I saw him in my mind's eye pulling the wrapping paper off one of his presents, he was so excited with his little tail wagging. I cried silently to myself as I held him as these memories flooded my mind. I didn't want him to hear me crying that night, I didn't want my holding him that night to distress him in anyway, even though my heart was utterly breaking knowing that I couldn't take him with me. I didn't have children, so consequently my little dog was my baby and had been for 13 years. He brought great joy to me every time I looked at him during our life together; I felt a deep love in my heart for him.

He had his head on my shoulder and my face was against his beautiful soft furry back. In my mind's eye I saw him sat next to me watching cruft's on the television, he loved cruft's and he loved football and snooker. I saw him in my mind's eye taking all the doggie toys out of his basket looking for his favourite orange spiky toy, and when he found it he played with it for ages. I saw him burying his little doggie biscuits with his nose in the corner of the room, thinking I couldn't see it any longer. I saw his biscuits hidden all over the place. I saw him following my ex-husband all over the garden as he mowed the lawn, and barking at the lawn mower.

Scene after scene flowed through my mind as I held on to him, I felt like I was in a complete nightmare having to leave him. I whispered to him how much I loved him and how much joy and happiness he had brought into my life, I thanked him for all of the love he had given me, I held onto him and I never wanted to let him go, then I put him down with a few doggie treats into his bowl, then I quietly went and drove away.

I drove a few minutes away from the vicarage. It was a very cold, wintery January night. I parked up and just sat crying for hours not knowing where to go. I didn't want to drive to my parents as they are elderly, and I didn't want to bring such trouble to their door. So I went to my friends home, a clergyman and his wife, long term friends of my ex-husband and I. When I arrived at their front door I could hardly stand up as I knocked on the door. On answering the front door my friend got hold of me and took me to their settee in the kitchen, I could hardly speak, all I can remember saying was "Jesus help me, Jesus help me" as the enormity of the situation washed over me.

I was utterly exhausted. That night I had lost my husband who I loved, my dog who I adored, my home, my church family, financial security and soon after my job. My friend just held me as I leaned on her shoulder sobbing. I was utterly broken. Everything felt so unreal; I couldn't believe this was happening.

Chapter 7

What could a "National Care Policy For Clergy Spouses and Children" In Marital Breakdown Look Like In the Church of England?

Housing is tied to the clergy post, which means the clergy couple do not own the vicarage. That fact in itself is a very insecure fact for a clergy spouse if a clergy marriage comes to an end. The clergy spouse is then told SHE/HE/CHILDREN must seek alternative accommodation. Some are given short notice to leave their homes, it all happens very quickly, leaving some clergy spouses and their children homeless. Some have a second home which the clergy spouse moves in to but then a little way down the line that home is sold as part of the assets to be divided. Some clergy have a home the clergy spouse and children can move in to and stay in permanently. Some spouses have adequate finances to get a mortgage for a home for themselves.

Knowing this experience personally and from the inside of the system, I would say clergy couples need an information session as part of the ordination process on what will happen if the marriage ends. It is too easy for a clergy person to send away a clergy spouse and children out into the world with no safety net; this is completely unacceptable and cruel behaviour from clergy people. Both the clergy person and the system need to take responsibility for the well-being of the clergy spouse and children if the marriage should break down.

The clergy person on marriage breakdown needs to take shared responsibility straight away in the care package of the clergy spouse and children. The reality is the clergy spouses are often left to sort this out on their own. We all know that moving to a new house is a stressful experience; under these conditions it's another huge pressure on top of everything else that the clergy spouse is expected to organise. Going through this stage is so difficult. On the wages I was getting at that time the rental figure I could afford was at the lowest end of the housing market scale. The first house I went to see was tiny, dirty and on an estate with great social challenges. It felt like a nightmare that this could be my living reality now. The next place I saw was a small one bedroom flat, again in an undesirable area of another town. I went to see these places alone because I felt humiliated and ashamed and very sad at my now only option living conditions. I had never had to live like that in my life and it was a scary option for me, but the only independent option. I had asked the Bishop's Visitor if there would be any help of temporary accommodation for me from the diocese, but the reply back from the Bishop was "no, there was nothing available". I was given no practical help from anyone in the diocese; I was totally left on my own at that time initially post separation, to sort living arrangements out. I had no secure financial means at that point. My experience is far from unique within "Broken Rites".

A contract should be in place that is drawn up at theological college making the clergy person aware that should a marriage breakdown occur at any stage of their marriage, that they will be part responsible and supportive for the care package, funding and making sure the spouse and children are in a safe home of their own. No clergy person should be allowed to set a time limit on the clergy spouse and children leaving their home, making them homeless. If they do set a time limit, living in the vicarage any longer after that is suggested, is practically impossible.

We are talking about the church here with Godly principles and practices. Clergy people going through separation and divorce should not be allowed to stand up in church on a Sunday and preach love, while dealing in the background in a harsh, unloving way to the clergy spouse and children. I must stress again that the clergy person also needs to be proactive in making sure the clergy spouse has adequate accommodation, and the clergy person to pay part of the rent or mortgage for a few years, until the clergy spouse is totally financially buoyant again. The clergy person should also as a matter of course pay maintenance for a period of time to the clergy spouse and children.

A spouse leaves their home, family, friends geographical area in support of their clergy partners vocation, so their well-being if anything should go wrong in the marriage, should to be assured.

When a marital breakdown occurs the following steps need to be considered:

- First of all a mediator should be assigned to the couple, and counselling should be offered to the couple **together** and apart if needed, to see if the marriage can be helped toward reconciliation. The couple need to face this situation together and be counselled together at times. Counselling is offered but to individuals not together.

- The Bishop should speak to all involved, not just the clergy person.

- If in the case of a marriage breakdown involving a third party, both couples, the four people should be interviewed by the Bishop to ascertain the truth of the situation, taking away the possibility of someone lying to a Bishop and being believed. Each person should be allowed to tell their story to the Bishop enabling the Bishop to clearly see the whole story not just one person's side of the story. If the four people were interviewed together the truth would surface very quickly because to lie to a Bishop is like lying to God and not many people would ever do that when face to face with all concerned. In many organizations for instance education, if a complaint is brought about a teacher, everyone involved is spoken to individually. When people agree to lies or lie about a situation or person they are destroying people. Decent people do not lie about others or agree to lie about others regardless of the pressure they may be under.

- Once the hierarchy have the whole story then action should be taken, and decisions made in disciplinary procedures if necessary.

- A mediator or safe guarding officer should be assigned to the couple to make sure living conditions are adequate for the spouse and children.

- The mediator or safe guarding officer should also make sure that the spouse and children are adequately provided for financially by the clergy person. If a third party is not involved to oversee these issues, the spouse and children face an uncertain future at the mercy of the clergyperson. I have read enough accounts now and had many discussions to know that these points all need to be covered. There are issues and situations going on, right now, today, for clergy spouses that make me feel sick to my stomach. I know all these issues can be sorted out well if other people are drafted in to make sure all concerned are working together to safe guard all involved. This will not cost the church further finances, as Bishop's Visitors and Safe Guarding Officers could be briefed on covering these safe guarding issues. Unfortunately because these issues are not being handled well by the church we are having to resort to legal advice, and no one wants to go to these lengths, but certain spouses have to follow this course now because of the very serious lengths some clergy people are willing to go to.

- I just want to digress onto an unrelated but very important issue as finances have been mentioned here. The Church of England is available for us all. The church conduct baptisms, weddings and funerals for all, regardless of whether we attend church or not, and these duties to us all are precious services for all involved. Please consider the following and please do not be offended. When the clergy at the end of these services remind people of the offertory box at the back of church, please don't think all the church want is your money. Please consider the following: the churches are open and funded by the congregations which many of these are small congregations. Many congregations are made up of elderly people especially in rural areas and villages. The congregations are funding all that the church needs, to stay open. When churches have events they are often well attended by many people in the community, and the church are always grateful for the generosity of the community in supporting those events and helping raise funds for the church buildings and projects. It would be great that just as a matter of course we could all bear in mind that, when we attend the baptisms, funerals and weddings, that our financial contributions are greatly needed and well received. Please give generously and know you are helping to keep your local church open.

- Back to the safe guarding and "National Care Policy" Considerations

- All safeguarding measures at this stage need to be adhered to.

- The statement of the marriage breakdown that goes out to the church/s should never be written by the clergy person (we have evidence of this happening). The statement should be the work of the couple, senior clergy person and mediator for safeguarding measures, so that the statement is a truthful one.

- The church congregation should never be told that the spouse and children have left the vicarage if the clergy person has made the decision to end the marriage, because, the flock will automatically presume the clergy spouse is to blame for the marriage ending. A high percentage of clergy marriages that end, are at the decision of the clergy person.

- The clergy person should never tell lies about the spouse to cover their reasons for ending the marriage. This will further safeguard the clergy spouse and the children.

- The best possible way forward should always put the children as a top priority. If a clergy marriage breakdown is handled in an incorrect manner, this will have a detrimental effect on the children emotionally, psychologically and spiritually. We must protect the children at all costs because if we don't, the children will carry great burdens into adulthood as they often think they are to blame for their parents troubles. The children need affirming and assuring during this transitional period, not counselling sessions that may label them and be on their records forever, a label they do not need. All they need is love, assurance, care, warmth and a safe passage through their parents troubled time.

- The way clergy marriage breakdown is handled by the church system at the moment is inadequate, and it could be so much better for all concerned. If it was handled in a more loving and caring way, the following could also be worked on. When the breakdown is handled so badly by the church, the percentage of clergy spouses and children who then do not attend a church any longer, is a high percentage. The spouse and children need to somehow find a church family that they can be part of again. I was invited to three different churches when my marriage broke down. I decided to go to the church where no one knew me apart from the pastors and the person who had invited me. This gave me space during the grieving process and my transition in life at that time. I went back to church very quickly because I did not want to be a statistic of high percentages of clergy spouses going through marriage breakdown that no longer had the strength to start again in another church. When a person has been abandoned by a clergy person and hierarchy it is very hard for the spouse and children to trust a church system again. Fitting into another church family is very difficult and often impossible. At the first hint in a new church of church politics and difficulties the spouse will then often retreat away. The biggest issue that destroys and halts growth within a church is gossip. I would encourage you to do your own study on gossip, it is an issue that God actually despises. It is very serious and detrimental to the church. God's ideal for the church is to love others and to treat everyone well and with respect at all times.

Clergy Safeguarding

When clergy are dealing with adult parishioners going through vulnerable times in their lives such as marital difficulties, separation, divorce, the loss of a loved one, the loss of a job etc, the clergy need to follow safeguarding measures and minister to the vulnerable parishioner in two's.

Chapter 8

The Bomb of Love

In the bible we read that faith, hope and love are very important in life, but the greatest of these is LOVE. I live my life one day at a time. I learned this lesson many years ago when suffering from an illness that had prevented me from having children, and another illness that had caused me great pain for many years as I was wrongly diagnosed. I went through a period of time where I forgot what it was like to live without pain. I had to find a way of dealing with that constant pain, so I learned to take "one day at a time". What that meant in reality was to forget what had happened yesterday, and not to worry about what was going to be happening tomorrow and just to get through the day as best as possible.

Whatever you are going through, try to take "one day at a time". You are going to need to be so strong as you move from stage to stage in your process. Clergy Spouse in difficulty please contact "Broken Rites". www.brokenrites.org We will help you through every stage. We all go through difficulties and challenges in life; my encouragement to you is "One day at a time".

A very important lesson we can learn from our catholic friends about illness is that not only do we share in the joys of Christ, but we also share in the sufferings of Christ. Suffering unfortunately is a part of life and accepting this can help us at times. Suffering in whatever form begs the question that everyone asks: "Why does God allow suffering? "Suffering and healing is a mystery. Why are some people healed and some people not healed? I don't know the answer to that question; but during all of the different stages in life I've chosen to trust in God at every turn. That has not brought me everything I've expected in life, but it has brought me a great sense of peace. We all suffer shock and great challenges in life at times but as we trust in God, we can live in and experience a great sense of peace the majority of the time. Difficult seasons in life can lead us closer to God or back to God and into a place of deeper peace.

Just suffice to say at this stage, I believe God Is Love, and there are some questions and situations in this life and world that are a mystery and may well remain so until we come face to face one day with Jesus. God looks at each one of us through the eyes of love. But each one of us has our own free will: we are not robots. We all as individuals choose how we are going to live our lives. For instance, if each one of us who are able were to sponsor a child who is hungry and lives in poverty through the organisation "Compassion", we would be helping to eradicate the hunger of children across the world. We have the power in our own hands to help change many areas of suffering in our world. www.compassion.org

Albert Einstein Wrote the following letter to his daughter Lieserl.

"When I proposed the theory of relativity, very few understood me, and what I will reveal now to transmit to mankind will also collide with the misunderstanding and prejudice in the world.

I ask you to guard this letter as long as necessary, years, decades, until society is advanced enough to accept what I will explain below.

There is an extremely powerful force that, so far, science has not found a formal explanation to. It is a force that includes and governs all others and is even behind any phenomenon operating in the universe and has not yet been identified by us. This universal force is LOVE. When scientists looked for a unified theory of the universe they forgot the most powerful unseen force.

Love is Light, that enlightens those who give and receive it. Love is gravity, because it makes some people feel attracted to others.

Love is power, because it multiplies the best we have, and allows humanity not to be extinguished in their blind selfishness, Love unfolds and reveals. For Love we live and die.

LOVE IS GOD AND GOD IS LOVE

This force explains everything and gives meaning to life. This is the variable that we have ignored for too long, maybe because we are afraid of Love, because it is the only energy in the universe that man has not learned to drive at will.

To give visibility to Love, I made a simple substitution in my most famous equation. If instead of E = mc2, we accept that the energy to heal the world can be obtained through love multiplied by the speed of light squared, we arrive at the conclusion that Love is the most powerful force there is, because it has no limits. After the failure of humanity in the use and control of the other forces of the universe that have turned against us, it is urgent that we nourish ourselves with another kind of energy.

If we want our species to survive, if we are to find meaning in life, if we want to save the world and every sentient being that inhabits it, Love is the one and only answer.

Perhaps we are not yet ready to make a Bomb of Love, a device powerful enough to entirely destroy the hate, selfishness and greed that devastates the planet.

However, each individual carry within them a small but powerful generator of Love whose energy is waiting to be released. When we learn to give and receive this universal energy, dear Lieserl, we will have affirmed that Love conquers all, is able to transcend everything and anything, because Love is the quintessence of life.

I deeply regret not having been able to express what is in my heart, which has quietly beaten for you all my life. Maybe it's too late to apologise, but as time is relative, I need to tell you that I love you and thanks to you I have reached the ultimate answer!"

Your Father Albert Einstein

LOVE IS GOD AND GOD IS LOVE

ARE WE READY TO MAKE A "BOMB OF LOVE"?

The church is the place to model LOVE to the greatest depths and degrees. The church embraces all groups and members of society. The clergy spouses have shown much love to all parishioners. We sacrificed much for the good of the congregation; and we were happy to do that. We were many times at the bottom of our spouse's priority list, but that is part of the sacrifice.

When clergy are ordained they make promises before God that they will be the "cure of souls", the translation which is better rendered today is "care of souls", taking care of the souls of the flock at all times. This is a huge and very important responsibility and one of which we know cannot be fulfilled perfectly at all times by any one of us within any relationship and family "all have fallen short of the Glory of God".

I as a clergy spouse at the time of my ex-husbands ordination service was only watching that service in the cathedral, but inwardly I made those promises too. Not in the priests way, but as wife to care in my way for others. God wants us all to remember that He is a Holy God. Just take a second to think about what that really means. One day we will all stand before Him as individuals. Today is a new day; start again, each day is a new beginning. Every one of us makes mistakes, but we need to learn from them and not keep repeating them. God forgives us, but sometimes people don't and won't forgive each other. Romans 12 verse 18 "As far as it depends on you be at peace with everyone".

In these last days don't be surprised if hatred and lies are directed towards you in a way that you have never experienced before. It is the enemy of your soul's plan to destroy people. The scorpions of hell are now released on the earth with the one sole purpose of causing the deepest of destruction against mankind. If there is a situation in your life where a person or a few people are attacking you, that attack is from a scorpion from hell. A scorpion has a venomous sting. If there is a real evil battle in your life going on against you, cry out to God; He will help you. If you are a person who causes destruction to others, stop, and start afresh.

The situation may not change for a while, but know God is with you in your boat. See the waters of the storm around you becoming calm. Regardless of whatever circumstances you are going through, you can remain calm, or very quickly as you turn to God in prayer calm will come to you. There are two ways to face situations: you can be like a drama queen, making mountains out of molehills, you can plot and scheme; or you can remain calm. Firstly take the issues to the Lord in prayer; talk to a few friends who won't fuel the fire and who will pray with you. It's your choice. The second option will bring more peace and calm into your life than the first option. It's your choice.

The enemy knows his days are numbered, but as children of God we need to stay focused and get on with the work the Lord has given us to do. Whatever attacks from others happen to you in the future, recognise them for what they are: I say again, ignore them, give them to God in prayer, do not be derailed, and get on with the work the Lord has called you to do. Don't be distracted by these attacks; do not allow them to torment you from this day forward. "But they that wait upon the Lord shall renew their strength; they shall mount up with wings as eagles". (Isaiah 40 verse 31) If your heart doesn't condemn you, then neither does God. (1 John 3 verse 21) You may be going through difficulty, but if you keep your heart and motives pure before God, He knows that. He sees your heart; He sees your motives. "EL ROI","I AM The God Who Sees You". If you've strayed or gone off the best path for you, run back to God today. He will restore you.

The clergy spouses are asking for one thing for the future and that is an adequate Care Policy For Clergy Spouses (and Children) going through marital difficulties, separation & divorce. Where Are Our Shepherds?

Clergy person, did you shepherd your spouse and children and make sure they were safe and had provisions when they were "Set Adrift? Or did you help to set them adrift quicker? Or did you stand back and do nothing? Were you the Good Samaritan, or did you pass by on the other side of the road?

Shepherds in the Church of England, did you shepherd the clergy spouse and her or his children? Senior staff and hierarchy, did you shepherd the clergy spouse who needed your help? Did you speak to the clergy spouse? Or did you reject her or him and the children? "When I needed a neighbour were you there?" Or were you covering a clergy person and sweeping the situation away as quickly as you could without clearly hearing both sides of the story?

You have badly hurt many clergy spouses; many of these sheep of your flock were left and abandoned in the ditch of life. Were you even concerned along with the clergy person who "Set Adrift" the spouse and children? A little yeast works through the whole batch of dough. What I present are the facts. You can continue to close your eyes and heart to these facts, or you can choose to open your eyes and heart and do something about the great injustice and hurt that has been done to many spouses and their children. Many of these clergymen should have been disciplined and called to account, but you choose to protect them no matter what.

Clergy Spouse

Southern Province

"There are no words to my situation at this moment in time right now. These cover ups by the Church of England simply have to stop. I am writing an email to another Bishop to ask for a meeting as I have found male church leaders including wardens, the Archdeacon and my Bishop have given me no help, I don't trust any of them now. It does seem that the most important thing is to uphold the good name of the church at the expense of the clergy spouses. Is that what Jesus would do? Absolutely not!" Clergy spouses cannot be sidelined and silenced any longer. This book is an attempt to have our voices heard and to restore justice into this situation".

Chapter 9

Vision During The Divorce Court Hearing

As I write this book I'm leaving all heartbreaking details out, even though I have permission to use much information; I'm being very careful what I write in this book because our main aim at "Broken Rites" is to help towards creating an all-round adequate "National Care Policy". That's all we need for future clergy spouses and their children. From an eternal perspective this account of a vision I saw during one of my divorce court hearings will, I believe, bring much into perspective. Well actually it will create one of two opinions. Either it will be believed and bring much comfort to others, or it will be rejected and ridiculed by some people. I have only had three visions in my lifetime; this is an account of one of them. I will refer to my ex-husband as husband in this account. One day when I attended my final divorce court hearing, I was representing myself, as I had no funds for a solicitor. When this second judge asked questions and listened to my husband's solicitor and my explanations, she then gave us two options to end the marriage from which we had to agree on one of the options. She then said to me I would have to go into a room with my husband's solicitor and decide between us what option from the two we were going to choose and agree on. She then said to me that I had not to be pressured into an option that I did not agree with.

My husband's solicitor was putting a great deal of pressure on me as he tried his very hardest to get me to accept his option for our divorce. He was forceful and reminded me that he had been practicing law for nearly forty years and the option that he was offering was the best for me. It was the worst and most distressing option for me; I was under great pressure. His forcefulness for that option was due to his lack of understanding of canon law. His solicitor had got his client into a very serious situation; so then the solicitor was putting all of the pressure onto me to accept the other option.

I kept saying "no", I couldn't accept those terms. I thought I was going to have a heart attack at the pressure I was being subjected to from this powerful solicitor. I felt smaller and more vulnerable than I'd ever felt before. The reality of my situation at that time was, I was without a home of my own, on the poverty line, jobless etc and now this solicitor was badgering me and trying to force me into another situation that would have been even further crushing for me. How I held my own that day I'll never know - well I do know, it was by the Grace of God; but my body, with all of this further pressure that I was under, was now giving way, I was going under. My heart had been beating fast for hours that day. It was a complete nightmare for me. I just kept praying in my mind, "Jesus, please help me, protect me, rescue me". My friend was with me that day in the waiting room. At the previous meeting one clergy friend was with me in the court hearing room and my two pastors were praying in the waiting room as that previous hearing was going on.

Suddenly in that present discussion room, outside of the court hearing room, I suddenly saw the courtroom of heaven above this solicitor's head, right across the room. Suddenly Into my mind came the words

"I AM your divine attorney, I AM above the British law system, I AM above the church system. I AM above the world system".

At that moment this very powerful solicitor sitting in front of me changed. His power and he as a man suddenly shrunk before my eyes. The power he was wielding against me, I knew was a minuscule power in the presence of the power of God.

Into my mind came the reminder that I was a precious child of God. God the creator of the universe was bigger than everything, God was bigger than any worldly law system and God was bigger than any church system. I knew that the courts of heaven were looking on at my situation right there at that moment. I knew they were watching and listening, but what I knew at that moment was that God was in ultimate control.

The biggest impression that was then laid on me was that the courts of heaven were not for one side in this hearing and against the other side, but they were there watching and listening. God loves all people, but He does not like our sin. Instant peace came over me as I beheld this sight. Moments later the solicitor stopped badgering me. We then went back into the court hearing, and the judge dealt with the ending of the marriage situation in a very fair way. I will never forget that vision. When the hearing ended, as I thought about the vision, I was pondering one word, why did the word attorney come into my mind? It was a word that I mostly associated with America. In the UK I was only familiar with the words solicitor and lawyer. I looked up the word attorney in the dictionary; it said the following "Attorneys and lawyers are the same thing"

Why have I shared this vision in this book? I believe I saw and experienced a situation that spoke to me of a loving God; regardless of the situation, God watches and listens. "EL ROI" "I AM the God who sees you." I don't want this book to come over as the clergy spouses on one side and the clergy on the other side; that's not where I'm coming from at all, none of us are coming from that place in "Broken Rites". We just want a fair system during this plight.

Our society in places and during some situations has been built on the silencing of women. Women have had to fight for their rights every step of the way over the centuries. All I am doing by writing this book is asking for a fair system in the church, and for clergy spouses not to be looked on as second-class citizens. There are no second-class citizens in the Kingdom of God. God loves every one of us, but He is watching and listening to our every daily decision.

Our Eternal Place And Position Will Be Determined By Our Earthly Decisions.

Let me say that again "our eternal place and position will be determined by our earthly decisions". Many people and systems think they are powerful, but in the presence of God we are very small. God is only interested in the state of our hearts and how we have dealt with others in our lifetime. We serve a Holy and Just God. He is a God full of mercy even when we are getting it wrong. I can hardly even explain the enormity of what this vision revealed. God is a loving God who isn't against us. Regardless of what is going on, He loves us, and He wants us to love each other, and deal with each other in LOVE. I knew God wasn't for me and against my husband or vice versa. I know He stands and watches and listens until the appointed time, when we will all, as individuals have to give an account of our lives to Him, and Him only. This is the end of the court hearing vision account.

In the clergy spouse accounts sent to me, over and over again it was the same issues. One particular clergy spouse was sent away from the vicarage as her husband was having an affair. That clergy spouse was sent away HOMELESS with children. When I talk about homeless I mean homeless with no financial provision even for a rental, I mean a clergy spouse who has to start again from the bottom with no short or mid-term provision.

Many clergy spouses have to find new jobs in new locations. I wrote off for close to 200 jobs without success. My brother-in-law took a look at my resume/cv; he advised me to take my date of birth off it. I did that, and then secured the next job I applied for. My close friend Jacquie had also had a very similar experience to me in finding a job when she had relocated to the same town as me. Her background was in education; she was highly qualified as well, and she too had sent nearly 200 applications for posts before she was successful in securing a new position.

The clergy spouse who was homeless with her children went on to become a very successful leader in her own field. She has done, and is doing, tremendously well. Some spouses are still struggling so much financially and with rented inadequate housing, hardly able to make ends meet at times. My heart breaks for them. Many of the clergy are allowed to stay in their posts in their vicarages, and many also have a second home with their new partners.

Many are not subject to any disciplinary action, and some are promoted while nobody even asks if their clergy spouse is okay and managing. They are able to relinquish all responsibility and just put a clergy spouse out onto the street with no practical help or financial care from him or her. I am well into year 4 of this struggle without my own home. My story is not unique! I wish that it were. When pension sharing is completed, often the clergy spouse will have those finances for the future but no means to buy a house. A percentage of spouses are able to buy a home in time.

Chapter 10

A Prayer For The Children of Clergy Families

Joel chapter 2 "And it shall come to pass that I will pour out my Spirit on all flesh, and your sons and your daughters will prophesy, and your old men shall dream dreams and your young men shall see visions". The church is trying to show the world an example of perfection but look at every single person that God used in the bible. None of them were perfect. The people God used in the bible had a scandal on them: David, Moses etc. The way that we do church is going to change. We are going to stand up with boldness and passion. It's not going to be a Christianity that is discriminatory; we are going to go out and bring in the homeless, the widow "We are rejecting some of the harvest because it doesn't wear a suit and tie" (Marcus Rogers)

Church of England, you have thrown away a group, an army of people of passion, love and compassion, hard workers for the kingdom of God. You have rejected, abandoned and thrown away this group of clergy spouses and their children. If this situation was handled in a more caring way, these clergy spouses could continue being used in another family of the church. Also clergy children could be a bold and strong Christian group taking the gospel of Jesus forward in the future. If they see unconditional love metered out before them during a time of much challenge and upheaval in their own lives, this could set an even stronger foundation within them, to face hard challenges in the future, and equip them to be strong Christian people as they grow into adulthood. Instead they have been broken and crushed further, due to the lack of care, help and love that should be theirs at all times, through the good and the challenging times. Instead they are seeing some clergy who are cowards and who won't face this challenge of marital difficulty. They see adult clergy people cowering away from the overall responsibility of their family. They are also abandoned by the church family because there is no one appointed to step in and make sure everyone gets through this traumatic situation as best as possible. Does anyone in the church ask these children, teenagers and adults how they are coping or how they have coped?

Some of them see strangers, counsellors, instead of those adults in the church who they looked up to as surrogate aunties and uncles and grandma and grandpa figures. All of a sudden they are taken away from all these people and everything that is familiar. They are a forgotten group, when at one time they were loved by many in their church. Adults who are supposed to be representing Jesus should treat no young person in this way.

Through the collation of all the evidence for the book, it is clear that the greatest of the tragedies and safeguarding concerns due to clergy marriage breakdown, the greatest sadness is for all the children who are caught up and onlookers of this sorry state of affairs.

For The Teenagers And Adult Children of the Clergy Family

If you are one of the clergy family teenagers or adult children now reading this, on behalf of the church and system that abandoned you and let you down, I want to say we all at Broken Rites acknowledge your pain. we acknowledge your grief, we acknowledge your trauma, we acknowledge your sense of abandonment. I am utterly sorry that you have experienced this. But as a person who cares for your future wellbeing, as a Christian and as an ex clergy spouse, I want to say to you, that God wants to heal all your pain, God didn't cause you this pain, it was human error. Whatever hurt has been caused to you; please forgive those who let you down. You understand a great lesson from Jesus: while He was on the cross, He said "Father forgive them for they do not know what they are doing". Jesus wants you to forgive whoever hurt you through this process.

You were not forgotten. "EL ROI, I AM The God who sees you". He sees you; you are precious and very important to Him. He wants you to take your pain and everything that you felt when your parents' marriage broke down. He wants you to give that pain to Him and to feel the release in your heart and know deep down in your soul that you are loved with an unconditional love. He will never leave you or forsake you, NEVER. His love for you is permanent and secure; He looks at you with the eyes of love and an incredible amount of empathy, compassion and love. I'm sorry that some adults, who you looked up to and trusted, let you down; but it's time now to let that pain, hurt and disappointment go. It's time for you to be set free from the pain of the past.

I wish we could have a service of reconciliation and healing, where we could all be together. Please be assured there are many clergy who care for you very much, and their hearts will be breaking as they read these words, as mine is as I write them. I feel a great cry of anguish in my soul for you right now and I just want to hug you till all the pain of the past goes away. You did nothing wrong; none of what happened was your fault. I know you have greatly struggled trying to build a new life, trying to build your life back up. You may still be struggling as an adult. Please don't blame God or an individual or the church any longer every person is a fallible human being. Every one of us makes mistakes. Please forgive us.

I'm going to write a prayer for you now, precious child of the clergy family. You may want someone to sit with you and be with you as you pray this prayer, because the tears may flow. You may sob from the depths of your being, but know that if that happens, it is part of your healing process.

A Prayer For Healing

Please say these words aloud
Hear yourself saying them

Heavenly Father, I don't know fully why what happened to our family happened. I don't know why we had to go through what we did. I didn't understand it all at the time. But you know, Lord, what I have been through. You know all the struggle and pain and confusion I have gone through. You know why I go silent, you know why I rebel, you see me every day and you know how I'm feeling.

Lord Jesus, I open my heart to you now, and I ask you to flood my heart, soul and life with your healing presence. I bring every situation, frustration, anger, and every tear I cried alone to You now, and I ask that you pour your healing balm over my heart, soul, body and mind. I'm just going to sit here for a while and give you this pain (talk to him now and give him your major issues, the major incidences, the major days and stories, and know He is with you right now listening to you and caring for you with more love than you could possibly imagine)

Heavenly Father, I know it is your will that I receive healing and release from the pain of the past. I ask now for a supernatural inner healing in the mighty name of Jesus. Your word says that you have good plans for me, plans to prosper me, plans to give me hope and plans to give me a future. I am calling upon you now, and I know you are listening to me now. I am seeking you now and I know I will find you in this healing place.

I thank You for Your continuous healing presence in my life. One of the greatest prayers I ask you is, please give me peace; a peace and rest from the past that I may happily and excitedly walk into my new future with you. Lord, if the going gets tough on certain days, will you always remind me somehow that you are with me, and may I always remember that whatever happens to me today and every day, that there is nothing that can come my way that You and I cannot handle together. Help me to take One Day At A Time, and to make the most of everyday.

In time Lord, will you use me to help others who are in inner pain so that my experience may not be wasted, but used to alleviate suffering in other people? Put the smile back on my face Lord, help me to bring lightness and happiness into other people's lives. Help all those other clergy children and young people to heal also. Put your strong loving arms around them and me, and as a group, help us to make a difference in this world.

"For he or she who the Lord sets free, is free indeed" Amen.

Tell Your Heart To Beat Again

Danny Gokey

You're shattered
Like you've never been before
The life you knew
In a thousand pieces on the floor
And words fall short in times like these
When this world drives you to your knees
You think you're never gonna get back
To the you that used to be

Tell your heart to beat again
Close your eyes and breathe it in
Let the shadows fall away
Step into the light of grace
Yesterday's a closing door
You don't live there anymore
Say goodbye to where you've been
And tell your heart to beat again

Beginning
Just let that word wash over you
It's alright now
Love's healing hands have pulled you through
So get back up, take step one
Leave the darkness, feel the sun
Cause your stories far from over
And your journey's just begun

Tell your heart to beat again

Close your eyes and breathe it in
Let the shadows fall away
Step into the light of grace
Yesterday's a closing door
You don't live there anymore
Say goodbye to where you've been
And tell your heart to beat again

Let every heartbreak And every scar
Be a picture that reminds you
Who has carried you this far
Cause love sees farther than you ever could
In this moment heaven's working
Everything for your good

Tell your heart to beat again
Close your eyes and breathe it in
Let the shadows fall away
Step into the light of grace
Yesterday's a closing door
You don't live there anymore
Say goodbye to where you've been
And tell your heart to beat again
Your heart to beat again
Beat again
Oh, so tell your heart to beat again

YouTube: https://youtu.be/eUHRDCYnFfg

Chapter 11

Shepherds Who Have Responsibility And Power

Shepherds of the church, please help sort this problem out for the future. Please don't pass by and relinquish responsibility. When we have no one to help us we are told it's up to the law to sort things out. So we have to wait years for some of our personal items and finances to be sorted out. "Look after the widows and orphans". Why is that so important as taught in the word of God? Look after widows and orphans because they were the most poor and vulnerable group in society. The widows had lost their husbands and the children had lost parents. The clergy spouses have lost their spouse and home. We are aware of the Church of England documents about Valued Linked Loans, but that does not help those who have no means.

We need a policy set in place whereby the clergy person takes responsibility financially for the wives and children from the outset. Clergy wives and children should never be abandoned to the street. God knows the truth of every situation. Even when it's been twisted, misunderstood, added to, lied about, God sees, and He knows the truth.

We are now becoming more aware about narcissism and gaslighting character traits. Throughout the accounts there is a common, visible, easily recognizable thread of these traits from a percentage of clergy who are displaying these characteristics. This is very serious for the clergy spouse who has no control over what is being said about them, to the worst of lies being spread about them. When people get themselves into a corner for whatever reason, all kinds of things get out of hand and lies are spread. Fear creeps in; it is a horrible vicious sad circle. Many clergy spouses have been subjected to some people who have lied and presumed so much that the people who do that believe their own lies and presumptions are the truth, when they are far from the truth. I'm not going to go any further down this route: it's too complicated, and an area for mental health professionals. The clergy spouse gets no help when these situations are happening to them and around them. There should be restraining orders put out as a disciplinary process towards those who try to destroy the clergy spouse in this way. Some of the spouses have been subject to very serious damaging lies and this has also got to be looked at and dealt with. But many clergy spouses can't get serious issues sorted because there are not clear national procedures from one diocese to the next, and also those who could help are not listening.

Many accounts report that other professional people sent in official complaints to the Bishops when they saw abuse-taking place toward the clergy spouse from the clergy partner. Complaints sent in from top professional people including people in the field of law, education, the medical profession and parishioners, asking the Bishops to help and step in when injustice and abuse is occurring. People sending in these complaints have had to wait from one to three months for a reply, or no reply is given. It seems as though all respect has gone from some Bishops towards the clergy spouses.

These words are not my opinion but hard evidence and first-hand facts. We know how serious it is to put this kind of evidence into the public arena, but this injustice is so serious and needs rectifying for future cases. We believe that Archbishop Justin is a man of integrity and we believe he cannot know the extent of our plight. We appeal to him to help create an adequate "National Care Policy".

This book is part of an ongoing campaign; we will speak up until we are heard and taken seriously, because what we have experienced at the hands of some in the Church of England is very abusive, and it is ongoing. A number of the clergy people/husbands/wives behave like unruly children who have always had their own way and never been disciplined, who know they will not be held to account for anything they do or continue to do. Clergy spouses are at the mercy of that situation and often no mercy is shown to us.

So where do clergy spouses go when all this is happening, and nothing is being done to help us? The Clergy Disciplinary Measure (CDM) is there, as a safeguard for those in the church when serious matters need a hearing. Some of us were advised by senior clergy to put in official complaints against our clergy person partner, as we had clear grounds of complaint. The clergy spouses are going through so much turmoil at once that it's emotionally impossible to face putting in official complaints, when we have evidence that most complaints are rejected for many reasons, "unsubstantial evidence" being one of the reasons, when there is clearly concrete evidence. It's a detailed procedure and an emotionally demanding one for the person needing the help over an abusive clergy person. When you are living in survival mode, the last thing you want is to be dealing with an official complaint against a clergy person. It is very intimidating for the clergy spouse to be dealing in an official capacity with members of senior staff and Bishops. There is definitely a fear factor involved. Many clergy spouses, due to the abuse already metered out by the clergy husband, will have the least possible contact with the clergy husband because they know they are fighting a losing battle; if they cause any further upset to the clergy person, the consequences on the clergy spouse can come back fifty times worse on them. So they learn to be as silent as possible, an action learned by many clergy spouses in their marriages.

I understand why clergy spouses and their children stop going to church when marriages break down, and why they lose their faith in God. For those who have lost their faith in God, I want to say to you that it is the institution of the church, which has a problem; it clings to the clergymen/women in their closed circle and is less civilized to their partners and children. They are not clinging to a faith in God; they are clinging to a club, system, and organisation: whatever you want to call it. They are certainly not clinging to a faith in God, because if they as individuals were clinging to God, they would not treat people in vulnerable situations so heartlessly. If we profess to follow Jesus and have a faith in God, his characteristics will show in every area of our lives. Eternal perspectives need to affect every daily decision for every individual person who stands before us. We all definitely do make mistakes in life, none of us are perfect, but we hopefully learn from our mistakes. If we keep making that same mistake over and over again, year after year, decade after decade, we need to ask ourselves, why?.

God's principles and way for us all as individuals, are very simply stated in Luke 10:27: Jesus answered, "Love the Lord your God with all your heart, and with all your soul, and with all your strength, and with all your mind, and Love your neighbour as yourself." When we are unable to love our neighbour as ourselves we are poor in spirit. My parents always encouraged and demonstrated caring for the poor people around us and further afield in this world; as the bible says, the poor will always be among us, and we need to be mindful of those who are poor and treat them with the greatest respect. We are not above other people depending on our bank balance and position in life. We are truly blessed in life depending on our love to all people, not just those in our circle.

*"Jesus is coming back for a spotless bride. The representation of His bride on earth is the church. Jesus is coming a second time and He is coming back for a spotless bride not a bride covered in acne." (**Christopher Spicer**)*

Individual person going to church

Following other people's words is not enough. Jesus wants you to have a personal relationship with Him. Read His word the Bible and talk to Him in prayer as though you were talking to your best friend. He will lead and guide you; He will comfort you and be with you always. He wants our trust to be fully in Him, because you will be let down by some people in this life, but your inner relationship with Him will be secure and permanent throughout your life. Your relationship with Him will enable you to continue to trust in Him even when chaos enters your life. He will strengthen you in your inner being, and He will enable you to not lose hope, even in the most difficult of circumstances. Please choose to make the decision to have a strong faith in Him. No matter what happens in your life, continue to trust in Him, even when you don't understand why you are going through what you're going through.

You, like many others in this world, may be going through great loss. Whatever your situation, please continue looking to Jesus for your strength and help. If you do that, in time you will be able to become very strong inside, and no matter what comes against you in life, your faith will stand the test of time. Your faith in God will continue, and you will be amazed at the strength you will have for very difficult situations in your life.

I am a nobody in the eyes of this world. I just live my life one day at a time continuing to trust Jesus with everything. But one thing I know, I know that by His grace I have a great faith in God; I know and believe that Jesus died on a cross for the sins of the whole world. I know Jesus gave not just part of His life for us, He gave His whole life for us all. He sacrificed everything for us, and I love Him for that. As I said, I am a nobody in this world, but I KNOW I am a precious daughter of God. I know we are all very precious and special in His sight. I know He knows our heart and our motives, and I know He knows, I try my very best in this life to live for Him and love and care for others. As I've recently just written every one of us have failed at one time or another, but His forgiveness is available to us all.

Clergy spouse and anyone else reading this book now, if for whatever reason through a life circumstance you may have lost your faith, I ask you right now to take your eyes off the one or the few of the circumstances that have deeply hurt you and look into the eyes of love. Jesus will never hurt you or leave you or desert you, NEVER. He wasn't the reason things went wrong in your life. Each one of us is responsible for the love in our heart, and we have the choice to love and care for others or to hate, hurt, ignore and destroy others. Can you find it in your heart to forgive those who have hurt you? Because if you can, you will be free, and they will have no hold over you. Do not be afraid of their threats, presumptions and lies; do not be afraid, because God knows your heart. You will stand before Him at the end of the day, no one else. Love and care for others with eternal perspectives, not worldly perspectives, in mind. The Lord has reassured me that I am covered by a canopy of His love and glory. I believe His canopy of love and glory covers everyone we bring to Him in prayer. His canopy of love and glory covers us all. Some of us know that, and some of us don't know that yet. Know you are special to Him, "EL ROI, I AM the God who sees you". He sees you even when you feel very alone at times, HE SEES YOU, and most importantly HE LOVES YOU. That in itself is enough to motivate us to love others. We are human and let ourselves down at times, but when that hurt towards others, that turning away and closing our eyes and ears to their need continues, what is that? It is far away from the love that God wants us to show to one another.

The Beatitudes

Matthew Chapter 5

"Now when Jesus saw the crowds, He went up on a mountainside and sat down. His disciples came to Him, and He began to teach them, saying: Blessed are the poor in spirit, for theirs is the kingdom of heaven.

Blessed are those who mourn, for they will be comforted. Blessed are the meek, for they will inherit the earth. Blessed are those who hunger and thirst after righteousness, For they will be filled. Blessed are the merciful, for they shall be shown mercy. Blessed are the pure in heart, for they will see God. Blessed are the peacemakers, for they will be called children of God. Blessed are those who are persecuted because of righteousness, for theirs is the kingdom of heaven.

Blessed are you when people insult you, persecute you and falsely say all kinds of evil against you because of me. Rejoice and be glad, because great is your reward in heaven, for in the same way they persecuted the prophets who were before you."

Chapter 12

A Message To Church Congregations

In future, if your clergy spouse suddenly disappears, please find out what has happened. Churchwardens or other church leaders please go to the clergy spouse; find them and help them. Talk to them, one to one; do not listen to any second-hand information. Please help and support them if they need you to. Don't allow the clergy person or system to cover this dilemma up any longer. I was desperate to have members of my church family around me. I needed you, but I had to stay silent.

Congregational friends

The spouses stay silent for a few reasons. Some clergy spouses are advised that they do not need to share with anyone in the church what has happened. The other reason clergy spouses stay silent is because they do not want to create a situation of "the vicar said this, the vicar's wife said that".

The clergy spouse will not say bad things about the vicar to you because we care very much for you, and your faith in God is of paramount importance to us. Please find us and stand alongside us. Do not turn a blind eye. Insist on a few of you getting our contact details. If God lays it on your heart, act. We didn't get to say goodbye. Our hearts yearn to see you and you may have felt abandoned by us, but we didn't abandon you, we had no other choice.

A Word For Pastors' Spouses in the USA

I received a word in prayer about a few particular States in the USA: Utah, Texas, Alabama and the USA in general. This word was heavy on my heart. I have personally been to the USA many times, and I love your country and understand much about the church systems. I know also that you have much support and there are organizations for pastors' spouses going through marital breakdown. We want to reach as many clergy spouses and pastors' spouses as possible before the marriage breaks down. We have a great deal of knowledge and experience, and we want to reach you before your marriage gets to breakdown stage. If you need us please contact us www.brokenrites. org. Also, search out your local organisation that supports pastors' wives. Clergy spouses, Pastor's wife, don't go through this alone; it can feel so isolating. Don't be alone in your difficulties.

If you contact Broken Rites, your enquiry will be dealt with in the strictest of confidence. Even if your husband is in a senior role or a well-known name, don't be in isolation; there is support for you. One of the purposes of this book is to raise awareness, so that no spouse continues to be in isolation. Nothing you tell us will be unique to you, and that is so great to know; that although you may be in very sad circumstances, there are spouses who have been through, or are going through, exactly what you are going through. If you are going through marital problems at any stage, we have representatives in the UK, USA and Europe.

If you are a spouse outside of these territories we do not have representatives in your territory yet, but we are here for you also. We love you and we care for your well-being and the wellbeing of your family. We wish so much that there were no need for organizations like ours. We wish with all our hearts that all marriage difficulties could be sorted out, and most of us would have done anything to make that a possibility; but sadly, the reality is that some marriages break down. We are here for you. www.brokenrites.org

Clergy Spouse

Southern Province UK

"I have had to go to outside agencies for help, as the church would not help me. The Citizens Advice Bureau has been helping me. I have decided to speak out now and to tell people that the Church of England seem to care very little about clergy wives, and I spell out my treatment by them, and people all say, "that's absolutely disgusting and unbelievable by a so-called Christian establishment". We need practical action now; I hope it doesn't take another 35 years."

Chapter 13

Marcus Rogers "A Prophetic Word"

1 Peter 4 Verse 12

"Do not be surprised at the fiery trial you are going through."

Joel 2. "You shall receive power after the Holy Spirit has come upon you". God is raising up a generation that have been hidden, they are going to come out and they are going to be bold and the world is going to be shaken. People are going to be asking, "How did they become full of Joy? How did they become full of Peace? How did they get the strong attitude that they have?" People are going to say, "I want it, show me!" and you will tell them, "It is through intimacy with God, it is because of the grace and the mercy of God, it's because of who He is, that we have what we have inside of us".

There is going to be a unity under the banner of Jesus Christ. People will not be able to deny the power, the heat and the anointing of the Holy Spirit. God is going to tear down a false perception and Jesus is going to wipe away all of the hurt and false perception. Those who are proud will miss what God is saying to the church in this day.

God is about to raise up people who have been in the wilderness, who have been going through great trials. God is saying, "NOW IS THE TIME TO RISE UP". I know that you've been in the cave, hidden away; I'm calling to you to rise up. I allowed you to go through the fire so you can be on fire, I allowed you to go through the wilderness so you can appreciate the Promised Land. I allowed you to go through this process because I was trying to shape you".

God is saying, "I want to be in control so that you can walk by faith and power and know that I will never leave you or forsake you. You will know that I AM the Alpha and the Omega; I AM the beginning of your life and the end of your life. I AM the beginning of your decisions and your choices, relationships, tests, trials and the storm, and I AM the end of it. I AM in full control, and when you truly understand that and believe that, you will go out and be bold and be not afraid".

The church is tolerating things that God would not tolerate, complying with things that God would not comply with. It's going to cost someone their job; it's going to cost some people their marriages. They're going to be people who have the Job mentality [Job was a brave godly man in the bible]. The Job's comforters mentality will consist of people who will look at your life and see what you're going through and tell you that you are false because you wouldn't be going through what you're going through if you were a true man or woman of God.

The reality is you are going through such trials because you're a threat to the kingdoms of hell. God is using you so the enemy is storing everything that he can to try to discourage you, to try to take you out, to try to water down your fire. You have to sit there with the mindset of Job.

Though they slay me, I will trust Him
Though they fire me from my position, I will trust Him
Though they lock me up, I will trust Him
Though they talk about me, I will trust Him
Though they divorce me, I will trust Him
Though they deny me, I will trust Him
Though they attack me, I will trust Him
Though they try to silence me, I will trust Him
Though they lie about me, I will trust Him
Nothing will put out my fire
Nothing will put out my desire
Nothing will put out my joy
Nothing will steal my peace;

I am more than a conqueror through Jesus
Christ. (Romans 8 verse 37)

Greater is He that is in me than he that is
in the world. (1 John 4 Verse 4)

No weapon formed against me shall prosper. (Isaiah 54 verse 17)

There is a separation that is coming. Casual Christians will become casualties. This separation is going to accelerate and is going to happen quickly.

The power and fire of God is going to pour out, and if you have one foot in the church and one foot in the world you are going to miss what God is doing now. Some of you are being cruel to God's anointed. None of us have God all figured out. We need to be very careful in what we say; we need to be very careful. No one is perfect; no one has all the answers.

There is only one that is perfect and that is God. God is looking for a people that are focused on him that are aware of what is going on in the world. Every person that God used in the bible had a ton of mess in their resume, but God said, "I will use you despite you". That is an amazing testament of His grace and power. We don't need to look a certain way or be a certain way for God to use us; that is pride and arrogance. God resists the proud but gives grace to the humble.

Chapter 14

Support From Others Towards Change

The Very Reverend John P Chalmers, who has been involved in the Board of Ministry in the Church of Scotland, spoke to Broken Rites on "Changing the Culture Which Leads to Abuse"

John explained that in the mid 1990s, his post had involved him in giving support to clergy families. One of the problems he had met was the fact that minister's families in difficulties do not admit to needing help. He was made aware of situations where no intervention to save a marriage was possible, as is the case for many members of Broken Rites. In most cases, the wife and children had to leave the home, which subsequently raised a whole range of issues. He said he had been a committed supporter of Broken Rites as long as he has been involved in pastoral ministry. He has promoted recognition of the work of Broken Rites amongst the clergy of the Church of Scotland and has been involved in making arrangements for the support of estranged wives.

His work has posed two questions:

1. Why are women left in such a vulnerable state by the church?
2. What cultural shifts are required to change this?

The short answer to his first question was that predominantly men run the church. Women become invisible to men in power. The answer to the second question was highlighted in a Christian Aid workshop on "Gender Justice", where it was made clear to him that the world is not so much 'maladjusted' as 'male-adjusted'. He described the situation in South Sudan, which is torn apart by war, and where women are abused and ignored. The key to peace in that region lies in the hands of the women who are at the sharp end of practical living. The men there, and in the church, need to face up to themselves and their attitudes towards women. This calls for an Act of Repentance; an acknowledgment of the 'sins of the fathers'. For this reason, he encouraged members of Broken Rites to continue their support for clergy spouses, and to work for radical change of attitude, which is needed in the church.

Archbishop Justin Welby, on a separate issue to this, said, "The reputation of the church, the reputation of a person, the reputation of an institution is as nothing compared to the call to obey God in Jesus Christ in the way we love and care for people. Everything that goes against that will in the end destroy the Church."

We also need to explore the issue of safeguarding around a marriage breakup for the spouse, children and reputation of the spouse. On the safeguarding issue, Archbishop Justin was recently quoted as saying "that he was 'open' to further funding of safeguarding across the 42 dioceses, acknowledging their diversity, and pointed out that this had already increased by £7 million. He confirmed that he had no formal safeguarding training before he became Bishop of Durham in 2011 or Archbishop in 2013. This has since changed and in 2014 he announced that he would not be willing to consecrate a diocesan Bishop unless they had already undergone safeguarding training.

The Very Reverend David Lunan addresses Broken Rites: "When Faith Makes It More Difficult". David observed the abyss of deception and betrayal, which he had found when meeting clergy families in breakdown. In Broken Rites he had discovered a group of people who had weathered the storm and survived, for whom the church should be providing, but does not. He spoke of the crisis of faith when God is silent as everything falls apart. He observed the sense of guilt that "I must have done something wrong". For many years before a breakdown in marriage, the spouse wonders "what am I doing wrong?"

This was a common thread throughout the accounts I received.

I must take this opportunity here in this book to personally thank Rt Hon Frank Field MP for all the work he has done for decades for Broken Rites. Thank you for your work, support and listening ear. I hope one day all your hard work will pay off, and we will have a secure and acceptable clergy spouse and children's care package nationally in the Church of England and all denominations.

Clergy Spouse

Church of Scotland

"The Church of Scotland has a good system in place safeguarding spouses of clergy. To begin with, I contacted Housing and Loan in the Church of Scotland offices. They are obliged to find suitable housing. I was very blessed and was able to choose my house! There is a trust fund you can apply to, and if successful, it can go towards furniture. Also there are charities that have a start-up pack for folks like us. There is a lot of support, but you need to know who to ask. The Church and the leaders were very helpful and caring towards me. The Church my ex-husband is minister of didn't help me."

Chapter 15

The Church of England On Marriage And Remarriage

In Christian marriage, saying your marriage vows in front of God is classed as a sacred institution. When a clergyman/woman decides they want a divorce for whatever reason, the marriage is over. The clergy spouse has no say, so after this decision is made there is little or no support or help in trying to reconcile the couple. Counselling support is offered but there is no talk of helping the clergy couple to get through their difficulties. This was the case for many clergy spouses.

Henry VIII showed the seriousness of a man/king in power at his treatment of his wives. When Catherine of Aragon failed to produce an heir for Henry VIII, he wanted to divorce her, but as we all know the Pope would not give permission for this divorce. So, for Henry to get what he wanted, he broke away from the Vatican and made himself head of the Church of England and was then granted the divorce by the Archbishop of Canterbury in 1533. The Archbishop was under great pressure to do this, but this is an example of the lengths some will go to for their own way regardless of the pain to anyone else.

The Church of England's Position On Remarriage

"Remarriage is always allowed if the couple's former spouses are dead. The matter becomes more complicated if one or both of the exes is still living".

The Church has had a clear stance on the subject of a Christian remarriage since the General Synod meeting of 2002. In a vote concerning marriage after divorce, the outcome was 269 votes to 83 in support of change . The Church of England teaches that marriage is for life. It also recognizes that some marriages sadly do fail and, if this should happen, it seeks to be available for all involved. Unfortunately, as you are now aware, the accounts clearly show that in many cases the church was not available for all involved. To think that a clergy person would lie to a bishop is inconceivable, but unfortunately some do lie to cover up the truth of the situation.

"Under civil law, clergy have the capacity to marry any two people (as long as the couple can legally marry). The Church advises clergy to think carefully before remarrying couples, and to ask them questions to find out how committed they are. The final decision rests with the clergy member.

The Church's suggested questions, concentrate on the intentions of the couple, and whether allowing the remarriage would be harmful to anybody involved:

- Does the couple understand that divorce is a breach of God's will for marriage?
- Do they have a determination for the new marriage to be a life-long faithful partnership?
- Do they seem willing to explore and grow in the Christian faith?
- Has enough time passed since the divorce for everyone to have recovered, and are there complicating factors from previous marriages (court proceedings or child support payments, for example)?
- Has either of the parties been divorced more than once?
- Was their relationship a direct cause of the breakdown of a previous marriage?

In the accounts and conversations I've had with clergy spouses, the facts are that when the clergy remarry, some of the above have not been adhered to. The reality is that at times they have left a 'car crash' behind them, and an ex-spouse still dealing with the pain of betrayal, grief and loss of faith, and that their children are also experiencing pain. More destruction is brushed under the carpet and reality ignored.

There has to be a degree of reconciliation of the situation, and a degree of forgiveness and repentance where needed, to allow the ex-family to move on with some kind of acknowledgement of the hurt and betrayal they have experienced, at the hands of a clergy person.

As difficult as a marriage breakdown is, the clergy person needs to also take responsibility for the spiritual fallout that will affect their spouse, children and wider circle. The happiness and healing of all concerned must be taken into account.

Our statistics show that a very low number of spouses end the marriage. Statistics also show a clear pattern from clergy people who often show the same characteristics and behaviour as each other when pushing their spouses away at speed.

Truth and honesty in these situations would bring quicker healing for the clergy spouse. When lies are dominant, the pain continues.

Broken

(Anonymous)

I sit before you Lord totally broken
Wondering how I will ever get through this
I have used your word on so many occasions
To help in all kinds of situations
I know all the best verses
All the comforting reassuring verses
That I have found in the past and
Felt totally reassured by
My heart has never been broken like this before
This situation has totally devastated and broken me
Like nothing ever has before
Nothing comes close to the great loss
I am feeling in my heart right now
I am going through the day
Trying hard to keep focus and to
Keep on joining in with others
But my heart is totally crushed
I don't know how I am ever going to
Get through or recover from this.

I don't know how I am going to
Even get through tomorrow
I have been faithful to you
I know you have given me a gift of love for others
I would never intentionally hurt another soul
But the one closest to me has broken my heart
My life seems like an empty space without her
I can't believe this has happened
I can't believe I will have to live my life
Without this other person
Surely this can't be happening
But it is

"Where can I go from your Spirit? Where can I flee from your presence? If I go up to the heavens, you are there; if I make my bed in the depths, you are there. If I rise on the wings of the dawn, if I settle on the far side of the sea, even there your hand will guide me; your right hand will hold me fast". Psalm 139 verses 7-10

Clergy Spouse

Southern Province UK

"When the divorce reached its completion I struggled with wearing my wedding ring, as it had been part of me for many years and I did not wish to lose it. I considered myself still married in the eyes of God despite the church's support for divorce. A female vicar friend of mine in the diocese suggested that I continue to wear it to remind me to pray for my former partner every day. Sadly when I met the Bishop this advice was overturned, and the Bishop insisted that I should remove the ring and move on".

"Those who think there is a time limit when grieving, have never lost a piece of their heart"

Chapter 16

Further Quotes from Clergy Spouses

"I was left without a home or finances".

"I had to start again from the bottom with no help".

"I was hungry one particular day and had no money; I nearly went into the grocers to ask for 2 oranges for free".

"My phone was turned off many times as I could not afford the rental charge at times".

"I had a £600 overdraft, which kept me going many times. One day I reached the limit, so the bank took my overdraft away, the safety net for emergencies was gone. I felt so low that day and the reality of my poverty hit me".

"I wasn't able to buy one new item of clothing for 3 years until I received a grant from Sons and friends of the Clergy".

"When on Universal Credit I often only had £13 to £17 per week for food".

"I had to move out of the diocese and begin a new life, leaving behind all my friends and family in the process. I also lost my job as I was working in the same diocese as him".

"My losses were so great, not just one major loss but several all at once. My daily life and struggle were beyond words. I felt like I didn't have the strength to live any longer or the will. In a haze of deep grief I planned how and the hour I was going to end my life that day. I knew exactly where I was going to go to end my life. When you get to that stage in your life you are not thinking about anyone else at all and how this action will devastate their lives. All you can think about is a way out of the pain. You detach from reality and you're just in that other place. In my final hour two friends contacted me. One by email with the most incredible treat to happen in six days' time and the other friend by text with a creative invitation for that evening two hours later. My friend wrote, "If you can come along, I'll pick you up in two hours". Their kindness in the space of ten minutes somehow clicked me back into reality. I knew I had to stay alive. They don't know; but they saved my life. I went along to the creative event, I felt very strange inside and close to tears all evening. I did cry at the end of the evening. That thought and planning process to end my life never came into my mind again. Three days later I started to rise rapidly out of that desperate deep grief".

Clergy Spouse

Northern Province

"What do you do about someone you've loved and trusted who then betrays you?. When a partner dies or a partner leaves you and ends the relationship for another person you're supposed to be able to mourn their loss, you're supposed to be able to grieve, but some are robbed of this natural part of the journey. In these situations, there is only one thing left to do: inwardly say goodbye and let go".

Chapter 17

Recognizing Narcissism

"Power Corrupts", not all of the time, but some of the time. We have all worked for a boss who uses the skills of all the employees in a wonderful life-giving way. We have also probably worked for a boss who is controlling to the last detail. Whether it's a boss or a manager, all in authority are to be listened to; that is part of the package as a leader or head of an organisation. But there are some who take their role to the extremes in business, family or organizations and become uncomfortably controlling.

In the church, the leaders are held very loosely accountable. They are trusted to get on and do the job well, like people in any organisation who are in senior management. We are trusted with great responsibility and expected to drive projects forward, sensibly monitor the financials and look after the staff.

Throughout many of the accounts I have received, a controlling nature is very evident in some of the clergy people. These controlling tendencies are more than controlling, they are narcissistic. Until a few years ago I had not heard of that word and looked up the definition. A narcissistic person does the following: frequently demeans, intimidates, bullies, or belittles others. I was very shocked when I read the definition as, throughout these accounts, clergy spouses had been subjected to narcissistic environments - there was a clear thread of controlling behaviour from their clergy partners. I was utterly shocked and very saddened when reading these clear cases of abuse. The abuse that many of the clergy spouses and children suffered or were suffering ranged throughout all the major abuse headings, emotional, psychological, physical, spiritual, mental and financial abuse. My heart was breaking as I read these accounts and, at this point, I wanted to run away from this project to write this book. The cries of the Israelites reached the ears of God and then He acted, but not until He had warned Pharaoh over and over again. We know the story.

Some living conditions for the spouses before separation became so difficult that a percentage of clergy spouses did not want to be a clergy spouse any longer. A small percentage left, others stayed for longer than they should have, but were honouring their marriage vows.

My friend Jackie recently said, "The name of Jesus is so powerful, we cannot fathom the magnitude of the power! When I call for HIM I believe it resonates in Heaven like a loudspeaker. Decree to be FREE. Let that be your mantra. There is no time for any ungodly power to rob you of your precious days left to serve on this earth. Decree to BE FREE!"

What happened to me personally was for a much bigger reason than just two people going through difficulties that ended in divorce, as sad as that was. I write this book for the sole purpose of knowing that God has heard the cries of the clergy spouses and most importantly, so that children will never in their lives see their mothers treated so coldly and without compassion by their clergy husbands and senior staff. I must stress again, this is not all hierarchy who turn away from clergy spouses, but a percentage of hierarchy who have to deal with a clergy spouse going through this plight, do not deal fairly.

My apologies to all in the Church of England who deal fairly with the clergy spouse and children - thank you so much. Please now join us in our petition to ensure that every person who goes through this plight can receive vital support.

The cries of the clergy spouses and children are too much and have gone on for too long to be ignored any longer. We learn to recognise the Lord's guidance and His warnings. The Holy Spirit witnesses to our conscience and if we take no notice of those warnings, there are always consequences. We can choose to ignore those warnings, or we can choose to listen to them. We will all have personal experiences of this. There are consequences to all of our decisions. His leadings and warnings are his guidance to us to help us. God's grace, compassion and love for each and every one of us are so great regardless of our failings.

One of my biblical heroes is Jesus' earthly father, Joseph. God guided Joseph in dreams, just like God guides many of us through dreams. What I love about Joseph is that he recognized the guidance of God in his life. As soon as Joseph had a dream from God, he IMMEDIATELY followed through on what God had revealed to him. As individuals, we can choose to ignore God's guidance and we can choose to ignore God's warnings, but if we do ignore warnings, it will be to our own detriment.

I understood fully for the first time why, for instance, Jonah ran away from what God was asking him to do. He looked at the culture of the day and the spiritual climate and his first reaction was to run away. When I began writing this book, I was personally still dealing with my own grief through all the loss I had experienced. So now on top of all of that, I was receiving all these accounts from clergy spouses, and in the accounts the clergy spouses were pouring out their own journeys of great hardship and loss as they were steering over uncharted waters and territories. Not only personally, but also for their children. At times, I had to take a few days away from these accounts as I collated the evidence I needed for this book. The pressure was great upon me as I read their experiences. I had asked the clergy spouses to send me their stories as factual as possible - not in an emotional way. Lawyers, solicitors, hierarchy want only the facts of your situation so try to cut out the emotional side of your story. The emotional side of life is impacted greatly when facing abandonment, homelessness, poverty and starting again.

As stated, the impact of all of these accounts on me personally as I was reading them and processing the information was huge. I was internally shaken for many days after reading some accounts. I felt very vulnerable and weak and sometimes physically sick, but I knew I had to carry on.

When you lose your own power through a controlling person, it is very difficult to get that control back over your life. But you have to, as I have already stated, there are no first-class Christians and second-class Christians or people in this world, we are all the same in God's eyes, He has no favourites. TAKE BACK YOUR CONTROL TODAY.

One of the aims through this book is to reach as many people as possible that are being abused emotionally, physically, psychologically, mentally or financially. I want people to recognise these holds others have over them and to break these chains. I don't use this word often or regularly but when people have these holds over you, these holds come from the pit of hell and are evil. God wants you to be free and liberated from these strongholds. No one should be abused in these ways.

How To Recognise If You Are In A Controlling Relationship

Answer these questions to help you discern if you are dealing with or living in an abusive situation.

- Does the other person shout at you a lot?
- Do you have to justify yourself to them?
- Do you have to do it their way all the time to keep the peace?
- Are you suffering from great sadness at their treatment towards you?
- Are they making you feel inferior to them?
- Do they comment on things and make you feel useless and worthless?
- Do you jump when they come into your workspace or home?
- Do you feel on guard around them like you have to give them your full attention?
- Do you have to attend to everything they say immediately, or they will go on and on at you until you do what they command?
- Are you afraid of them at times and for that reason do you do everything they say?
- Do they make you feel as though you are not good at anything?
- Do they say bad things to you and have no remorse for those words or actions?
- Do you feel as though they do not want you near them and do they deliberately upset you so you will go away from them?

- Do they pour cold water on your happiness?
- Do they not see the ninety-nine things you have done and point out the one thing you have not done?
- Do you go silent around them as a protection for yourself?
- Have you learned to be quiet and silent around them?
- Do they ever say anything good about you in company?
- In company when you speak do they ignore your comment and go on to another topic of conversation?
- Do you make mistakes in front of them because you sense the pressure from them to be perfect?
- Do they undermine you in public?
- Are they cold and hard hearted towards you?
- Do they say bad things to you and about you?
- Do they celebrate you or do they just tolerate you?
- Are you answering yes to most of these questions?
- Who is this person who you are thinking about right now?
- Say their name out loud, write their name down and look at their name.
- Take stock of your answers.
- Do you need to take action and protect yourself?
- What are you going to do about that relationship or friendship?

I saw these traits over and over again in the accounts I was reading. Clergy, ministers, pastors spouses and anyone else reading this list, if this list is ringing alarm bells for you and you have told no one and you're dealing with your life in secret, it is time to speak up.

If you can't do that with anyone in your circle of friends, please contact an outside agency. Anyone else outside of clergy circles reading this book speak up now, if you don't know where to turn contact women's aid or a male equivalent agency.

No one will tell you what to do; they will just listen to you and help you find advisory people who can help you in your situation if that is what you want and need. Don't be alone in this whoever you are, and whatever your situation is - whether it is in the home, workplace or wherever. Whether you believe in God or not, He believes in you and wants you to be free from every type of abuse. If you are going through any form of abuse you may be in tears right now. I'm speaking to both men and women: dear friend, seek help now and get this sorted out. I know abuse in any form is difficult to face up to and deal with, but once you do and you then seek help you will be free. Jesus came to set us free in every area of life.

Those questions I have asked you are to help you to discern if you are in a place of being abused. Whatever form of abuse you are going through, bring it out into the open. GET AWAY FROM TOXIC PEOPLE IN YOUR LIFE THAT DON'T CARE ABOUT YOU AND YOUR WELL BEING, WHO SAY BAD THINGS AGAINST YOU, GET THOSE PEOPLE OUT OF YOUR LIFE. PROTECT YOURSELF AND YOUR CHILDREN IF NEED BE. SURROUND YOURSELF WITH PEOPLE WHO CARE FOR YOU AND WANT THE VERY BEST FOR YOU. Let the dross rise to the surface now, this is your time to face up to the truth and reality of your situation. When you face up to very difficult circumstances you may feel physically sick, this feeling may last weeks or for a month or so, don't be afraid of your bodies reactions, THESE REACTIONS WILL GO AWAY IN TIME. Presumptions and lies are also forms of abuse, if you have been on the receiving end of them let me remind you EL ROI "I AM THE GOD WHO SEES YOU". God sees you, He hears you and He wants you to seek the help you need, so do not be concerned about what people think or say. The main thing is that God sees and hears He wants the very best for you; so don't be afraid.

Break Every Chain

Tasha Cobbs

There is power in the name of Jesus
There is power in the name of Jesus
There is power in the name of Jesus
To break every chain break every chain break every chain
To break every chain break every chain break every chain
There is power in the name of Jesus
There is power in the name of Jesus
There is power in the name of Jesus
To break every chain break every chain break every chain
To break every chain break every chain break every chain

There is power in the name of Jesus
There is power in the name of Jesus
There is power in the name of Jesus
To break every chain break every chain break every chain
To break every chain break every chain break every chain

There's an army rising up
There's an army rising up
There's an army rising up
To break every chain break every chain break every chain
To break every chain break every chain break every chain

I hear the chains falling
I hear the chains falling
I hear the chains falling
Break every chain break every chain
Break every chain

Chapter 18

Safeguarding And Tied Housing

As already stated, in Australia, the number of clergy spouses who stop-attending church after their marriage breaks down is 93% - a high percentage also lose their faith in God.

In Broken Rites we have spouses whose faith has stayed strong in God even through their very difficult circumstances. We have those who don't go to church any longer but still have a faith in God. We also have those who don't attend church any longer and have lost their faith in God. Also, there is a small percentage that didn't go to church or have a faith in God. A marriage breakdown is brought about by people's error, not God's error. Why do we blame God for all that goes wrong in the world and in our little world? If we take a step back from the situation, we can clearly see that man's power, decisions and choices create great difficulties and hardships in this life - nothing to do with God.

God's comforting words into all this mess is "Out of every evil I will bring forth good". Out of every situation we go through, God can and will bring good out of our situations, out of your situation. Life gets very messy at times and can get very difficult. When my marriage ended, my friend Jackie came to me with a bible in her hand and said, "all the promises in this bible are for you now". I chose to believe them.

As adults going through the mess of separation and divorce, we have had a lot of life experience behind us to draw from and understand. For children (and I have touched on this issue in a previous chapter, but I want to unpack this a little further) this is a different matter. What was your faith experience as a child, teenager, young person? Put yourself in the shoes for a few minutes of a child/teenager going through clergy family breakdown. They see and experience the whole spectrum of their parent's breakdown, then wherever they come on the priority list of each parent, plus the church response to them and their sense of abandonment on a few major fronts. Then having to leave the vicarage and starting again wherever, under a cloud of hurt and confusion. A high percentage of clergy children who go through this experience lose their hope in the church system, also they lose their fragile trust and hope in God, and for many this stage for them goes into adulthood. Many of the children witness and go through abandonment from the church and establishment. It's just so heartbreaking.

"Do not cause one of these little ones to stumble" This should not be happening; a care policy needs to be in place for them too. Not a heavy ended counselling policy but a way to soften the blow for them and for the church to show them they still care about their well-being and assuring them that they are still part of the church family and system; a very special part. They need to know that they are still loved by others and by God. They too are abandoned and this needs to be addressed quickly.

The purpose of this book as I said at the beginning is to create an adequate "National Care Policy for Clergy, ministers and pastors spouses (and their children) Going through separation and divorce" The Bishop Visitor's role is mostly limited to a pastoral role. Someone needs the authority and power to implement action and temporary provision until each separate case is on a steady footing and until things are safe and secure around the family having to leave the vicarage and church family.

Provision has got to be made to assist in this transitional phase. The issue of Tied Housing is a VERY SERIOUS issue and needs to be addressed as quickly as possible so that no other clergy spouse and their children end up homeless or living in poverty. Even temporary poverty is not acceptable. There should be a department of advisors, advocates, or mediators overlooking the provision the clergyman is making to the spouse and children. Making sure they are safe and cared for with basic human rights such as a home and enough money to live on until the financial settlements are finalized if there are any assets available. This department need to make sure that the clergy person is not feathering their own nest and taking as much as possible, leaving the clergy spouse and children with the least amount of financial assets. Unfortunately, this is what a percentage of clergy have done. These are facts with evidence. Please put someone in control of this aspect of care in our churches.

Each diocese needs to be following an adequate national care policy. Serious damage has been done to the clergy spouse and children in a way that they may never recover from; or take many years and decades to recover.

Away

Cindy L Spear © 2018

While the storms rage through your day
And the winds rise up in the night
As your ship is lost on the seas
And the shore is far from your sight

His beauty abounds in the wake
As He stretches His hand over all
Words of peace will come in the swirl
And the waves will suddenly fall
Cast it away to the wind

The cares, the turmoil of sin
Let His love lift your heart
Fill your soul with His light
Cast your fears away to the wind

For the power He has is real
As we wait on Him for our strength
We will rise on the wings of hope
Much stronger because of our faith
Though trials may come in this life
He will never set us adrift
As the tempest rages and howls
His promise of peace is our gift

Chapter 19

I AM the God of Miracles

Everyone Is Precious In God's Sight

Amongst all the deprivation and hurt, I have seen many miracles and God intervening in many situations and God's provision. In my next book, I'm going to write up my personal account of the miracles that have taken place. I'll write about one of those miracles at the end of this book. I learned to totally trust in His word that said, "I will provide your every need".

In God's eyes, we are all the same and are all as important as the other. God has no favourites; there are no first-class people and second-class people in God's sight. We are all equally precious and HE LOVES every one of us. EL ROI I AM THE GOD WHO SEES YOU

I cannot end this book without recognizing and acknowledging the pain that has been caused to other church members. We at Broken Rites (most of us are not clergy, but all of us as ex clergy spouses)

are interested in the well-being of every person in the church. The spiritual well-being above all is of paramount importance. Sorting situations out quickly that go wrong is very important if at all possible.

Church leaders are custodians of the flock. If one of the flock wanders away, like Jesus, we have to leave the ninety-nine and go and rescue the one and bring them back home. I say the following not as a judgement but as a fact. Leaders, clergy and pastors will be held doubly accountable. Why is that? Because you have been given charge by God of the safekeeping of the family of GOD.

Christ is the head of the church, you are under Christ's leadership over your denomination, you are under Christ's leadership over your diocese, you are under Christ's leadership over your archdeaconry or your circuit, or province, and you are under Christ's leadership over your church.

No wonder the word says leaders will be held doubly accountable. GOD has put every person in the flock into the care of your hands. We are all going to see Him one day. We are all going to stand before HIM one day, alone, to give an account of our lives. We will have no synod with us that day; we will have no chapter or deanery with us that day. We will have no team members with us that day. We will have no church system with us that day.

This isn't a business we are dealing with; these are souls we are dealing with. I bring to the table souls who have been very badly hurt and many still hurting through the effects of all the issues I have covered. Vulnerable people who are going through one of life's greatest sadness's: a marriage breakdown.

Please consider this account and please stand with us in our petition to create an adequate "National Care Policy" as soon as possible. Can we push this through and sort this out as quickly as possible? We don't want another clergy spouse and any other children to go through abandonment, homelessness and poverty. Each separate diocese needs to have a safety net in place and also the ability to see the spouse as God sees her or him. See them through the eyes of Jesus and act accordingly. Would you put your own wife, husband, son or daughter out onto the street with no provision? Hierarchy, leadership, in any denomination in which you are a leader, you are in charge of the spiritual security of your flock. Every one of them is precious in God's sight.

Please do not allow any of your leaders to hurt one of these little ones; they are God's precious children.

Beautiful Woman (Rap)

Femi Lloyi © 2018

To all the ladies preserved through pain
Through trials and tribulations finally respect again
I see your tears through your fears the pain left behind
I'm so sorry that you hurt I pray that you'll heal with time
You're a strong intelligent woman
And knows who's who and who's respect I'm giving
People are unaware not knowing what they have
But you're the mother of the earth and for you
I'm so glad
You're a beauty and a half
With every aspect of your worth
Despite the negative things you might have heard

You're the fibre that keeps families together
You're a living jewel?
And you've been perfected by the Perfect One
You're the hope of today and tomorrow
You're filled with dreams and promises
But yet you see sorrow
You're made strong through trials and tribulations
Which will become your crowns for elevation
You may fall but no one can hold you down
Salvation bring the Spirit and the Golden Crown
When I rhyme it is to break the
Shackles from your mind
It's the inside of your heart that's what makes you fine
Beautiful woman where does the
Secret lie in your heart in your mind
Your superwoman taken from the ribs of a man
Be brave because I say Gods bringing a new plan

Chapter 20

El Roi

"I AM The God Who Sees You" Part 2

I have thought long and hard about the following, as I am very conscious that I do not want to lay any blame at anyone's door; it is our job to love all, and God's job to judge. Some clergy spouses have the time, energy, stamina, hope and strength to make a better day for ourselves, work towards new businesses to help us recover from the poverty line and get back to building careers etc. Some of our members are not able to do that. When I read of them moving from rental to rental and the uncertainty in our lives where a home is concerned after the many decades of sacrificial service to their now ex clergy husbands, church and system, I am deeply saddened. Knowing the financial struggle day to day for a percentage of them and knowing there is not going to be a time when they can enjoy retirement without financial pressures on their shoulders is hard to process. If I had the means, I would buy those in that category a little home of their own, somewhere they can be at peace, without the constant pressure they are under. I understand that pressure, but know we have to trust God in all situations and not fret about the future - even when areas of it look bleak and unsettled.

I was at a retreat centre at one point working on this book on Easter Sunday. I was reminded of new life, resurrection, hope, renewal and new beginnings. I have worked hard on this book, sometimes into the early hours of the night, when all is quiet and still. I met a lady on the retreat - a stranger - who wanted to tell me something. She stopped herself until I encouraged her to speak to me; she said I wouldn't be interested in what she had to say. I felt sad for her and wondered what on earth it was that was so troubling her. It suddenly felt like the world and time were standing still. I said to her, "please tell me what you want to say, I'm listening".

She then went on to tell me that she was once the wife of a Wing Commander in the Army. Out of the blue, her husband said that he didn't want to be married to her any longer. She told me she was very beautiful in her younger days as she supported his calling to the army. She hosted many events for the army wives and was always there for her husband and the wider army family. She had been looked after very well by the army as a Wing Commanders spouse. After her divorce, and to this day, she lives in a council house and takes the bus everywhere, as she cannot afford a car. Her ex-husband has properties all over the UK. He managed to keep all of this out of the division of assets. He drives big 'flash' cars and lives a very comfortable lifestyle.

Did you make sure that your wife or husband was given the least amount possible? Did you have no conscience or genuine care for the well-being of your partner? Are you leading a flock knowing there is a trail of damage and destruction behind you? Do you have no care for your wife or former ex-partner and at times do you show a lack of care for your children? If so, you can, and need to fix this. Do you know that you may have crushed people with unbearable demands, and that you never lifted a finger to unease their burden when it was in your power to do so? Have you shut the door of the Kingdom of Heaven in people's faces? Have you ignored important aspects of life like Justice, Mercy and Faith? I say again, there are no first-class and second-class citizens in the family of God, which is why Jesus showed characteristics of a servant, to show us the way He wanted us to treat people. He took on the very nature of a servant. He is our role model; He had compassion on the crowds that followed Him. He is a Good Shepherd to every one of us. He loves us all equally.

Sometimes when things happen in life we are in danger of losing sight of God. This can be rectified. Don't fight against your conscience, put things right. The guilt will lift.

Psalm 46:10 "Be still and know that I AM GOD" I will be honoured by every nation. I will be honoured throughout the world. The Lord of Heaven's Armies is here among us; The God of Israel IS OUR FORTRESS.

Matthew 23 reveals why the religious leaders would want to crucify Jesus. They wanted Jesus out of their hair. Jesus was brutal in His honesty, and the religious leaders couldn't stand it. They just wanted Jesus out of the picture. Some Bishops, clergy, and senior staff just want the soon to be ex clergy spouse out of the picture, and out of the church city, so they close down on us and have a cold corporate attitude in their final email to clergy spouses.

I apologise again to hierarchy, senior staff and clergy who treat all people with love, care and respect. But some among you hurt and destroy, and this behaviour needs to be monitored and changed.

At the hands of those who have not shown love, care and respect, the consequence of that has now caused a simmering volcano within a group of people who have been treated very badly at their hands. They have closed many of us down when they don't even know us or understand the situation we are in. Consequently, this small percentage group of clergy who act the worst to the spouse and build up the most damning and damaging picture of the spouse continue in their double standard, double lives, and get away with it - leaving their spouse and children in dire straits for years.

The Lord of Heaven's Armies is observing all of this. We know that the Lord of Heaven's Armies is not against one or the other party, He has shown me this very clearly in the vision while in the divorce court hearing. He is not against one person and for the other person, No, but He sees all. He IS a God of Justice, Mercy, Hope and Love.

GOD IS LOVE and He wants us to show that love to a hurting world, one person at a time. This is the greatest aspect of our characters that He wants to shape.

We all know a few people who truly exude this genuine love. It flows from every pore of their being. They are only able to truly love to that degree because of His character that has been fashioned within their hearts and souls.

Chapter 21

Final Words

As I have already stated, it is not my intention or the intention of Broken Rites members to bring any detriment to any individual person or system, but to raise awareness of this very serious issue so that the outcome will be change. You have heard our plight.

It is in the power of the leaders in the Church of England (and all denominations) to create a safety net and bring change on this issue and to be an example to others in heading towards reform of this policy in the Church of England, quicker than is presently happening. Having a home to call your own is a Human Basic Right. Under the human rights charter, a home is a Human Basic Right. There are a number of basic rights that are being violated.

A percentage of clergy spouses did not expect to reach their age and be without a home of their own. I cannot see yet when that problem will be resolved for others and whether we will ever have a place of our own again that we can call our own home. When marriages break up when people are in older age, having to get a mortgage until they are 80 is beyond us.

I am aware of the work over the past few decades towards making life more secure for clergy spouses. I know enough to see that the wheels towards that aim are turning at a snail's pace. That concerns me greatly as we are dealing with people's lives here.

I hope we can form closer networks to alleviate the added pressure of clergy spouses and children going through this plight. We need a safety net for those in the future and greater help for those clergy couples in marital trouble.

The responsibility of care for the whole family on marital breakdown needs to be placed predominantly at the feet of the clergy couple. This needs to be overseen by a department working as Bishops Advisors to make sure that the spouses and children are safe and have a home to go to. This issue cannot be passed to the law system as some Bishops have advised to clergy spouses because, when the clergy spouse has no money, they cannot afford a solicitor to sort the finances and assets out. Some spouses have the greatest struggle on their hands through the lack of help and concern for their well-being. Men of God look after the vulnerable among the leadership families, do not allow anyone to be "Set Adrift" and got rid of in this manner.

Please implement an adequate "National Care Policy" and integrate a safety net for clergy spouses and their children.

I asked a number of clergy spouses the following Question: "What were the top issues that were your greatest challenges when going through the system of marriage breakdown, separation and divorce?" Here are a few of their answers.

Clergy Spouse 1

"Loss of my sense of identity and calling to the ministry of hospitality and supporting leadership.

The mental health of my child through the loss of stability in school and community (on top of losing the family, home, respect for their dad) and drastic reduction in circumstances.

My own mental and emotional health, bashed in by his adultery, which massively damaged further by the loss of my home, church, community and friends

The loss of faith in the institution I had made my life, but which has no integrity. This has given my children the opposite of spiritual nurture and moral guidance and treats my existence as an embarrassment - while whitewashing his misdemeanors.

The loss of housing security, despite the generosity of my elderly parents. I'm unlikely to get a place with enough space for future grandkids to stay".

Clergy Spouse 2

"It was very hurtful realizing that my ex's "colleagues" had no concern for me.

Wondering whether I could ever sing a hymn again without feeling deep grief.

Losing my future retirement years with the man I'd been with for four decades, with all our shared family memories.

Suffering long term worsening complex "Post Traumatic Stress Disorder" because of the speed and brutality of the divorce.

Losing my loved role in welcoming a big range of people into my vicarage home was a great loss".

Clergy Spouse 3

"I lost the right to live on the island. I became unqualified.

Previously I was only allowed to work because my husband was a Rector. He lost his job.

Moving out of the Parish was difficult. I was often invited to funerals or other services but had to ask the permission of the Dean to attend".

Clergy Spouse 4

"It was very difficult having to move from a home and town I loved living in.

Losing my position in society, a role I was told I was good at.

No money, only in a low paid job as we had moved so much. I always saw my role as supporting his ministry.

The rumor mill: "wasn't it sad that the vicar's wife left him" - this wasn't the truth.

On the positive side, I found my strengths and found out who my real friends were".

Clergy Spouse 5

"It was devastating losing my home.

Loss of identity and expected future life.

Loss of extended family - my in laws cut me off even though my ex-husband ended the marriage. He never admitted the affair but is now married to the other woman.

Lack of support and misinformation from church hierarchy.

Rumors and lies that I had never supported him and had left him. We had only been in this place 2 years, few people knew me as I worked long hours out of the parish. Previous parishioners recognized this as a lie but all too far away to give anything but long-distance support. I felt anger that his life hardly altered he even got promotion! While my life was destroyed. The anger came much later".

Clergy Spouse 6

"I had to cope on half income; this was only held together by me taking in a lodger - all whilst paying half of the University rent for both daughters.

My ex-husband manipulated the children by saying wrong things about me to them in order to save his own relationship with them. I did not do the same but am still suffering the effects of his deceptive behaviour years later.

Loss of identity as wife, clergy-wife and respected mature Christian in some circles.

Rejection, sexual rejection and the need to rebuild self-esteem after abandonment.

Loss of hopes, dreams, ministry, expectation, future life, comfortable retirement. I will need a mortgage until I'm 80, just to keep a roof over my head".

Clergy Spouse 7

"Having to move myself and my children out of our family home (the vicarage) and away from the community that was our support network.

People continually asking me if my husband was okay and if we were going to get back together, and me not having the freedom to answer those questions truthfully due to his misdemeanors being covered up.

Seeing him being given freedom of speech amongst the congregation to paint a false and favourable picture of himself whilst I was not allowed to tell the truth for fear of it upsetting people.

Him being given another job for a church organisation despite being married to me and clearly with another woman.

Trying to help maintain a good relationship between him and our children whilst he clearly had other priorities. My experience was not destitution but could have been if I had not somehow kept my very difficult teaching job long enough to pay the mortgage until the endowment matured. My husband 'gave' me the bungalow (with mortgage), which we had been able to purchase mainly with my income. It was meant for our retirement. So economically, my losses were not so great".

Clergy Spouse 8

"I had to carry on teaching Religious Education at the school in the same parish where my husband, as a local incumbent had been a regular speaker at school assemblies. The school was a large comprehensive 'Community College" (non-C of E)

After the divorce, he and his second wife, who had lived next door to one of my students, moved into another house also in the same parish, in the school catchment area.

My son was in the same class as the daughter of the second wife, from the age of 13 until 16. I feel this contributed to his social difficulties later. He was depressed for a very long time and still is not employed or in the 'system'.

Two daughters, one at the school where I taught, and the other where my son was, had to listen to rumors about the behaviour of their father and the name - calling. Both suffered in different ways with loss of confidence or rebellion. They have since 'come through' and made good marriages but hate speaking of the divorce.

The rector of the 'mother' church in which my husband served phoned me up to rebuke me for returning to the church the week after my husband had left. My head teacher and pupils of the school were in the congregation and the choir. I did not know why my husband had left - but the rector must have known. This is all the pastoral care I received at the time, apart from a two-sentence reply from the Archdeacon when I wrote to tell him of the Decree Absolute after a divorce process, which took 6 months. He wished me well in my 'new life'".

Further Account Information

The accounts show that often, first of all, the clergy person will undermine the clergy spouse to the parishioners, senior staff and hierarchy. This clear pattern demonstrates that they first questioned the mental state of the clergy spouse and put out doubts and rumors undermining the clergy spouse in this area. They then went on to undermine every area of the clergy spouse life - creating blame for the marriage break up on different areas of the clergy spouse life. They then undermined and morals of the clergy spouse.

What I now know is that the clergy spouse group are women and men who have achieved amazing things in life. Our group is a mixture of people who range from high achievers, academics, doctors, teachers, artists including, poets, painters, musicians etc. This group of people have shown great strength in the face of high opposition.

After reading accounts and seeing how people are coping and carrying on making new lives after such destruction has occurred, I feel immensely proud. I have never heard a victim mentality in these accounts. Being clergy spouses is a great training ground in dealing with difficult circumstances; we're not used to just dealing with our own small family unit - we were part of the congregation's lives and all that entails. Trying to make everyone feel equal in our eyes was integral to our role; we wanted to show that the congregation's issues were important to us as we prayed and walked alongside.

"Nothing is Wasted".

See yourself regardless of your situation as an eagle rising from the ashes. In time you will. To every person who has faced such opposition and abuse: as you face that pain without retaliating, be assured that God will raise you up from the ashes into a new place and into a much stronger person. His justification will come to you in many ways - including a greater sense of peace amidst the circumstances.

Prayer is NEVER wasted

Prayer strengthens us and gives us hope of a new day and draws us closer to God. Clergy spouse, I honour you for what you have coped with, for your integrity and strength and for what you are rising from. May God mightily bless you and give you "Double for your trouble".

Broken Rites Members

There is a great sense of love, care and unity amongst us through our shared experiences, and a great sense of love and compassion in our hearts for each and every one. I thank God for this. Much love and prayers to each and every one and thank you for your support and care towards me.

To you dear reader thank you for getting this far in the book. May God richly bless you, and remember He is with you in whatever situation you are going through. He will help you and always be there for you. Church and churches are a visible reminder of the presence of God among us. We will never find the perfect church because they are full of human beings and none of us are perfect. However, we can all gain much from being a member of a church. I am bringing to light a problem that needs to be faced and dealt with in a positive way, but remember I am referring to a small percentage of the church system but nevertheless an area of great concern and of which there needs to be a solution.

We can all receive a great sense of peace when we go to church and it is a great institution with some family difficulties. When we have family difficulties within our own small family units, if these issues are not dealt with they become bigger issues. In this instance we hope and pray that out of this serious difficult situation, the conclusion that will be reached in time, will be a new or revised "National Care Policy" for clergy spouses and children.

Chapter 22

Jesus Hand

Although this book has a very serious message that needs addressing, I just want to remind you that thousands of clergy marriages are thriving and very happy. The majority are fine, many senior staff, Bishops and clergy want to do the best for the flock - unfortunately, some have let us down badly in the system. No names have been mentioned and never will be - please keep in mind the percentages of clergy this has happened to. Although marriage breakdown is a small percentage, even so that small percentage is enough to warrant change and a complete review of the present care policy. We need change. Many or most systems in the world are going through great change and upheaval at this moment in history. The political system, the educational system, and the medical organizations - all systems are facing huge challenges at this time.

Again, I would ask you, don't fall into the trap of generalizing and pointing the finger and saying or thinking that all clergy are part of this story. Many thousands in the UK alone are people who love God and who love others and who give their lives to others, they sacrifice their lives for us all. Baptizing our children, taking services throughout the week, visiting the sick, the bereaved, being there for us through our joys and through our sorrows. Burying those of our loved ones who have died. They all actually work too hard for the good of us all and they put themselves at the bottom of their priority list for the good of our needs.

But over this entire human endeavour, human success and human failings, I want to remind everyone of us near the close of this book that God is the Head of the church worldwide. That Jesus' nature is compassion. We want to help the broken hearted - that is part of the character of Jesus. I want to remind us all ultimately that it is The Lord who has the final say over everything. In our busy hectic world, Jesus can easily get pushed to the edges of our lives, but the Lord is ultimately in control. He is the Alpha and Omega, The Beginning and the End, The First and The last. It is from Jesus where our ultimate help comes from. The first person we should take our needs to is Him. They said of Jesus when He claimed to be The Son of God, that He was either a lunatic or He was telling the truth. 2000 years later, millions of people continue to put their trust in Him and believe that He died on the cross for the sins of the whole world, that you and I might be forgiven. If you were the only person in the world, He would have still given His life for you.

As stated earlier, I have now started writing a book on all the answers to prayer I've received during these four years, and miracle answers to pray when I've got down on my knees many times and sought Him only.

2 Chronicles 7 Verse 14

If My people who are called by My name will humble themselves, and pray and seek My face, and turn from their wicked ways, then I will hear from heaven, and will forgive their sin and heal their land.

I want to tell you a final experience before I end this book, about an answer to prayer. At the beginning of my journey as a newly separated wife, some words were said to me that greatly distressed me - to the point where I went into shock and shook for a straight 16 hours. I had no sleep that night; I couldn't stop shaking due to the shock of those words. Later that day after the sleepless night, I drove to my friend's house. She was a calm, prayerful lady who had ministered to many people who had been bereaved and whose marriages had ended. I didn't say much to her; I just wanted her to pray for me.

She read some of the bible to me in her calm gentle way, and then she asked me if she could anoint my forehead with oil and pray for me, I said "yes". She went and fetched her little bottle of anointing oil, she dabbed her finger into the oil and wiped a cross with the oil onto my forehead. She then stood behind me and laid her hand on my head and she began to pray for me; my world was in turmoil. She prayed that the Lord would fill me with His peace and bring healing to my troubled soul. I then felt a hand gently slip off my head; it was instantly replaced with another hand, a huge hand. It was the right hand; I felt the fingers of this hand behind my left ear. The rest of the hand was resting all the way over the top of my head, and I could feel the thumb behind my right ear. I had my eyes closed and I said to my friend Jenny, "do you still have your hand on top of my head?" She answered me from the other side of the room and said "no". I told her what I've just explained to you. She said, "it is Jesus' hand, just be still and sense His healing presence".

She never said another word. All the shock started to leave me, my body that had shook constantly for 16 hours began to calm down, until all the shaking stopped. My head rested on the back of the chair and sunk back in pure peace. I stayed still just feeling the hand across my head. I could feel a pulse coming from the centre of the hand; I felt the heartbeat of Jesus through His hand, a gentle heartbeat. Then I felt the presence of the hand slowly disappearing until it was gone. I told my friend it had gone; she estimated it lasted 10-15 minutes.

She then gave me a blanket, I was exhausted; she covered me up on her settee and I went to sleep for 3 hours. When I woke up, my mind and whole body were at peace again. I've never shook since then. A few times soon after that when I had a few official meetings to go to about the separation, on the way to those meetings in the car I felt the hand very gently again on my head and, though not as pronounced as the first time, I felt the heartbeat. I experienced this on two other occasions in those early days. I knew they were tangible reminders that I wasn't alone.

The final thought on this story and a new revelation to me, is one I would like to share with you. My friend Jenny had her hand on my head but when she took her hand away, I was allowed to feel the hand of Jesus over the top of hers.

Here is the revelation:

When we pray for people and lay hands on them, Jesus' hand is on top of our hands. Let me say that again: "When we pray for people and lay hands on them, Jesus hand is on top of our hands". Trust enough to take your hand away and know as you continue praying for the person that Jesus' hand is on the person. When Jenny's hand was on top of my head, she in her faithfulness to God started that process, trusting that Jesus was going to help me and minister

to me. Then, when she had finished praying, she stood in the room with me - it was Jesus' hand resting on me until the healing came. We weren't in a huge meeting or in a church setting, we were in Jenny's sitting room. A faithful servant of Jesus willing to take time and pray with a hurting exhausted clergy spouse, a humble setting where a miracle happened. The accounts of the miracles of Jesus were amongst crowds or in small intimate settings. Jesus is only a prayer away.

You may have faced a crisis of faith in your life, or you may not have ever put your faith in Jesus. He is alive, He is real, and He wants you to know that He is in the boat with you; He wants you to know that He can calm the waters of your storm. You too may have experienced your life being "Set Adrift" over certain issues and situations. You may have lost everything on your journey, but even in your loss you too can have an understanding and experience that will deepen and draw you closer to Jesus. He wants you to discover His compassionate calling on your life. He wants you to have peace amidst your storm. He wants you to understand His great love for you. There is no peace in this world like His peace. It is my prayer that you will experience His deep peace. If you would like to start a friendship with Jesus

Pray this Prayer

Heavenly Father I come to you now, I ask you to forgive my sins and help me to turn my back on sin, and all that is not good for me in my life. Jesus I turn to you now, and I ask you to come into my heart and life and be unto me all that I need, that I may start a new life with you helping me. I believe you died for me, I believe you love me; I want to surrender my life into your loving hands today and I ask these things in Jesus Mighty and most wonderful name. Amen.

If you have prayed this prayer today, drop Jackie and I a little message at jackiebates@icloud.com and let us know, we would love to hear from you. It will be the greatest life-changing step you can ever make. Start reading your bible and have a talk with God every day. That's all praying is, just talking to Him, as though you are talking to your best friend. God wants us to fully trust in Him. For Him to be the number one person we run to, not phone a friend first, or ask the audience first, but to fully trust in Him first, and chat over the situation with Him first. Listen to Him, seek His guidance above all others. Everyday ask Him to speak to you through His word the bible, and to lead and guide you. Ask Him to give you his vision for your life and walk in your God given purpose.

Jeremiah 29 verse 11

"For I know the plans I have for you," declares the Lord, "plans to prosper you and not to harm you, plans to give you hope and a future. Then you will call on me and come and pray to me, and I will listen to you. You will seek me and find me when you seek me with all your heart. I will be found by you," declares the Lord"

I leave you with this quote:

"When the Japanese mend broken objects, they aggrandize the damage by filling the cracks with gold. They believe that when something's suffered damage and has a history, it becomes more beautiful."

God be with you always, He loves and cares for you more than you could ever imagine.

ABOUT THE AUTHOR

Vivienne lives in the UK. This is her first published book although she has written others. Vivienne is a singer songwriter, radio presenter and Children & Youth Ministry Advisor. Her albums and singles have consisted of solo work and collaborations and are available on music platforms worldwide.

Further information on future books and music can be found on her website. www.vivneville.com

Albums

Veiled In Mystery

Emmanuel

What A Friend

EP Advent

Christmas Collection (An Instrumental Collection)

Singles

Silent Night

Mary did you know

Breath of Heaven

What A Friend We Have In Jesus

Angels

Holy One

Let Me Know Your Presence

**Future Book By Vivienne Neville (2019)
EL Roi "I AM the God Who Sees You" Miracles
of God through the "Set Adrift" season.**

Vivienne Neville